Writing a
Successful
College
Application
Essay

Writing a Successful College Application Essay

Fifth Edition • George Ehrenhaft

BARRON'S

For Dave, Ellie, and Sylvia

About the Author

George Ehrenhaft, a graduate of Columbia College and Ohio State University, has helped students write successful college application essays for over three decades. He is the former head of the English Department at Mamaroneck High School (NY) and resides in Moraga, California.

© Copyright 2013 by Barron's Educational Series, Inc.
Prior editions © Copyright 2008, 2000, 1993, 1987 by Barron's Educational Series, Inc.

All inquiries should be addressed to:

Barron's Educational Series, Inc.
250 Wireless Boulevard
Hauppauge, New York 11788
www.barronseduc.com

Library of Congress Catalog Card No. 2012044341

ISBN: 978-1-4380-0149-4

Library of Congress Cataloging-in-Publication Data

Ehrenhaft, George.
    Writing a successful college application essay / George Ehrenhaft.— Fifth edition.
        pages cm.
    Summary: "An instructive guide to writing a compelling college application essay"—Provided by publisher.
    Includes bibliographical references and index.
    ISBN 978-1-4380-0149-4 (pbk.)
  1. College applications. 2. Exposition (Rhetoric) 3. Universities and colleges—Admission. 4. Academic writing. I. Title.

    LB2351.5.E37 2013
    378.1'616—dc23

                        2012044341

PRINTED IN THE UNITED STATES OF AMERICA
9 8 7 6 5 4 3 2 1

Table of Contents

GREETINGS FROM THE AUTHOR

Hello, and welcome to the world of the college application essay. Because you are reading these words, I assume that you're on the verge of applying to college or that you're already immersed in the process and are about to write one or more application essays.

Whatever your current status, this book is meant to help you write application essays that cannot fail. In these pages you'll find virtually all you need to know, in effect, to write your way into college.

I can't guarantee that you'll get into your first choice of college. But if you follow the guidelines spelled out in this book—from picking a topic to proofreading your essay—you're not likely to be rejected because of a weak essay.

Thousands of students over three decades have helped me to write this book. Many were students in my English classes. From their stumbling but sincere efforts to write essays of all kinds, I learned what it takes to make words clear, interesting, and correct. I also realized that most students work harder on their application essays than on any other writing they do in high school. Often for the first time, they saw that skill in writing could make a difference in their lives, that words empower them to disturb the universe.

Okay . . . maybe you've got a less lofty goal—like being accepted by your favorite college. If that's what you're after, you've come to the right place. The book's six chapters will show you how to write a potent application essay, one that will convince college admissions officials that you're too good to turn down.

I wish you the best of luck. I'm rooting for you.

George Ehrenhaft

Every college and university should ask prospective students to submit an essay as part of their application for admission, not only to underline the importance of writing, but also as a means of learning more about the needs as well as the strengths of students.

—A recommendation from
College: The Undergraduate Experience in America, a study of education by the Carnegie Foundation for the Advancement of Teaching

1   ADMIT? WAIT LIST? REJECT?

Step into virtual reality for a moment and seat yourself at the desk of a college admissions official. It's mid-January, the height of college application season. Seven days a week you're reading applications for next year's freshman class. Today you've read thirty-five applications. It's dark outside, your eyes ache, and most of your colleagues have gone home.

Before you can rest, however, you need to read three more files and write a summary of each applicant's credentials. You'll also rate each candidate—admit, wait list, reject—and via your college's paperless evaluation system, send your decision to the computer screens of the other members of the admissions committee.

Like most admissions counselors, you deplore turning down reasonably qualified students, but frankly, you have no choice. Applicants far outnumber the spaces available in next year's freshman class, so you must weigh the facts about each one, predict the impact that each would have on the life of the college—academically and otherwise—and make a decision.

> As an admissions officer, you carry an awesome burden on your shoulders—the destiny of real, live people.

All three candidates have filed a Common Application along with your college's supplementary forms. Jeff G's papers show that he's taken several honors classes in high school, including five AP courses. He'll graduate in the top ten percent of his class. You note also Jeff's 2100 on the SAT, and his involvement in school life as a yearbook staffer, cross-country runner, and co-captain of the debate team.

For his application essay, Jeff has chosen to discuss an accomplishment or event that marked his transition from childhood to adulthood. His response was uninspired—sort of dull, in fact. Jeff makes the point that various high school activities have helped him become serious-minded, industrious, and responsible. In college he expects to study hard and earn high grades.

Kathy E's application boasts that several achievements in foreign languages are central to her identity as a person. Kathy has won school awards for excellence in Spanish and French. She's also studied Mandarin. In college she plans to major in languages and hopes someday to work for the U.S. Department of State or the

United Nations. Her overall average is 90, and she's scored 1950 on the SAT. In school she joined the language clubs and helped to publish a foreign language newspaper.

Kathy's essay also contains a list of foreign countries she visited during the last two summers. It makes the point that travel has broadened her awareness of the world's diversity.

Pat McM's application shows that he earned an 86 average in the basic college-bound track of his high school. His ACT score is not distinguished but within the range for your college. Pat acted in several school drama productions, played the saxophone in both the jazz and the marching bands, and in the eleventh grade devoted considerable time to Students for a Clean Environment.

To answer the essay question about a time he challenged a belief or idea, Pat wrote an imaginary conversation with God after the Earth's ozone layer had been completely destroyed, and only a few humans were left. During their talk, Pat, devastated by the planet's condition, asks God, "Now that you allowed this tragedy to happen, why should I believe in you?"

Three good students, three qualified candidates for admission to your college. A high average and varied activities strengthen Jeff's application. Kathy's passion for foreign languages commends her strongly. Pat's commitment to outside activities compensates for his marginal numbers.

The majority of U.S. colleges would probably grab all three in a heartbeat, glad to have attracted such high-caliber applicants. But the more selective schools would screen them with agonizing care before deciding.

In the admissions offices at some colleges, committees employ a point system, assigning weighted numerical ratings for each candidate's academic and personal qualities. Two members might read and evaluate each file. Borderline applications might be passed around to a handful of readers for a group decision. At the University of Chicago, up to seven people have been known to read a single application.

Around the conference table, essays often serve as the wild card, the piece of an application that may give an edge to a student like Pat McM. Writing a conversation with God shows that Pat has the courage to take intellectual and creative risks. His approach is distinctive, and it confirms his interest in environmental issues. The fact that he wrote a dialogue may suggest that his drama experience has left an enduring mark on the way he thinks. In short, he put himself into his writing.

In contrast to Pat, Jeff G and Kathy E didn't. Both wrote proper but boring essays that could hardly be distinguished from countless others. Jeff's "what-I-did-in-high-school-and-what-I-learned-from-it" approach is common and uninspired. So is Kathy's conclusion. Kathy roamed Europe but brought back a cliché. By submitting dull essays, both Jeff and Kathy have tarnished otherwise sterling records and have jeopardized their chances of getting into a selective college.

Only 300 of nearly 2,000 four-year colleges in the United States choose their students with noteworthy rigor. During the last five years the most competitive colleges and universities, in fact, have turned away more applicants now than at anytime in their history. The reason is that many more high school seniors—close to two million annually—are applying to college. At the same time, the average number of applications per student has multiplied, in part because of an explosion in the use of the Common Application. Most students no longer labor over multiple applications. Instead, they fill out only one—the increasingly popular "Common App," and with a single click on their computer screens, mail it to every college on their list.

How Colleges Decide

While each college takes a slightly different path toward making admissions decisions, most of them quickly eliminate applicants who clearly can't do the work. "In general," says Muhlenberg College's dean of admissions, Christopher Hooker-Haring, "students do a pretty good job of matching themselves up with colleges." As a result, 85 to 90 percent are academically qualified and survive the first cut.

After checking grades and courses, some colleges turn to recommendations from counselors and teachers. Although most colleges ask you to take a college admissions test, the weight assigned to SAT and ACT results varies considerably from college to college. How you spent time outside of class may also be gauged because colleges seek students apt to participate in and help shape campus life. You'll be judged, however, not by the number of activities you've joined but by the depth of your involvement. Three years as a reporter or editor on the school newspaper will count more in your favor than several single-semester stints in five different clubs or organizations.

The reputation of your secondary school also matters. Colleges know which schools habitually send out high-achieving, energetic learners. In addition, colleges like a diverse geographic blend, often favoring candidates from distant regions of the country. An alumni connection within your family can help, too, along with a cordial interview with a graduate of the college or an on-campus meeting with an admissions official.

In other words, each section of your application adds another dimension to your portrait. If you are not a superstar like, say, a Merit Scholar or world-class swimmer, you'll end up in what Harry Bauld, a former admissions rep at Brown and Columbia, terms a "gray area." According to Bauld, such applicants are "in the ballpark" but still far from being accepted. Faced with large numbers of good scholastic records—such as those submitted by Jeff, Kathy, and Pat—admissions officials, therefore, make decisions using what Karl M. Furstenberg, former dean of admissions at Dartmouth College, calls "the intangibles," qualities that don't show up on a transcript and can't be listed in a résumé. And nowhere are such characteristics more evident than in your application essay.

In effect, the essay serves as a window into your mind and personality: Unlike an A- in chemistry or an 80 in English, it reveals your uniqueness—what you think about, what drives you, and what you aspire to. Naturally, it also demonstrates your writing ability. The gift of expressing yourself clearly, interestingly, and correctly can compensate for a weakness—such as a mediocre SAT or ACT score—in almost any other part of your application.

Typically, an effective essay can offset a mediocre SAT or ACT score.

In other words, an effective essay can set you apart from and above students with test scores and a school record similar to yours.

Why Do Colleges Ask for an Essay?

That's a legitimate question. After all, you've already written an essay for the SAT or the ACT Writing Test. Based on your grades in English and other courses that require essay writing, colleges ought to be able to deduce a fairly accurate picture of your writing ability. Yet, you've been handed still another essay assignment. Why?

By requiring an essay or two, colleges are informing you that writing well is crucial, both in college and in life. Colleges are also telling you, "We want to get to know you as well as we can," and encouraging you to write an honest essay that will shed light on the distinctive person you are. But more to the point, they're giving you a terrific opportunity to show them why you deserve to be accepted at their college. Admissions people everywhere say that grades, teacher recommendations, and test scores count heavily, but in an essay—aptly called a "personal statement" on some applications—you can project a clear sense of who you are, what turns you on, what you stand for—what makes you tick. The essay, in fact, is the only place on the application where you have the freedom to put yourself front and center. As Dean Hooker-Haring of Muhlenberg puts it, the essay enables you to "reach out and grab an admissions officer by the lapels and say, 'Here I am! This is why I belong at your college!'"

> Colleges want essays that show them the distinctive person you are.

Essay assignments differ from college to college. More than five hundred institutions, among them Boston University, Ohio, Wesleyan, Cornell, Mills, Loyola, Hood, and Holy Cross use the Common Application (or "Common App"), which requires a single essay written on one of five topics (fully explained in Chapter 2). More than half the Common App schools, however, want a second or even a third essay written in response to questions on their own unique supplemental applications. Case Western Reserve, on its supplemental application, asks for two additional essays. Others, such as Denison, want three short essays no more than 250 words each. Brandeis, William and Mary, Duke, and many other schools offer optional questions, some to be answered in a single paragraph or less. "Yes, they are truly optional," Duke applicants are told. "If you choose not to answer them, your chance of admission will not be affected." That may be true at Duke, but skipping an optional essay may be a gamble at other colleges. Rensselaer designs essay topics according to applicants' college majors. Prospective engineers write different essays from pre-law students. Supplemental essay questions often relate to such matters as your interests and goals, why you want to attend their school, and what you expect to contribute to campus life. Those applying to Lafayette must write an essay only if they haven't had an on-campus or alumni interview. Some colleges, such as Reed, Sarah Lawrence, and Bennington, ask applicants to submit not only an essay but copies of an analytical paper they've written for a high school class, complete with the teacher's comments and a grade.

In the college admissions process, a perfect essay—even if such a thing existed—won't compensate for less-than-brilliant grades or a transcript full of easy high school courses. Yet, a recent study by the National Association of College Admissions Counselors found that the essay ranks high among their criteria for admission. In fact, over half of the colleges give the essay "considerable" to "moderate" weight in admission decisions, just under SAT and ACT scores. Nicole Curvin, dean of admissions at Marlboro College, ranks the essay as the second most important criterion after the applicant's academic record—that is, after grades and difficulty of course load. At Bennington, Bryn Mawr, and Smith, where the essay carries as much weight as any other part of the application, some candidates, in effect, write their way into college.

Although finding your way into the right college may seem like traversing a labyrinth, well over a million students make the trip every year. At times the admissions system may appear fickle and unpredictable, almost beyond understanding. Yet, it works. As a college-bound student, you took your first steps toward your destination years ago when you learned to read and write and to compute numbers. You've studied, worked, and contributed in some way to your school and community. You've taken the SAT or ACT and established your school record. You narrowed your college preferences, and perhaps had an interview or two.

> In your essay, prove to the admissions staff that you're too good to turn down.

By the time you fill in your name on your first application, the facts about you—for better or worse—are in. You can't change them. However, the opportunities in your essay are wide open. In your answers to the essay questions you have the chance to shine brighter than your competition, to prove that you deserve a place in next year's freshman class. Let the essay work for you. The remainder of this book will show you how.

2 WHAT TO WRITE ABOUT

Before admitting you, colleges want to be pretty sure that you can write well enough to succeed in the courses they offer. They also want to know who'll be populating their classrooms and dorms. To that end, they've devised a means—the application essay—to learn about applicants' experiences, talents, character, personal philosophy, and zest for living. In short, the essay helps colleges decide whether you and their institution would be a good match.

Over the years admissions officials have made up countless essay topics. Lately, however, they've increasingly relied on the five topics found on the Common Application. By using the Common App, colleges, in effect, have done you a favor. Instead of forcing you to write a different essay for every one of the three, six, ten, or more colleges you apply to, you write just one essay and send it to all of them. Granted, some colleges require additional writing on supplemental applications, but unlike applicants of the past, you're being handed a one-time opportunity to write the single best essay of your life.

Common Application Topics

During the past year, roughly 700,000 college applicants submitted almost three million essays to 527 private and public colleges and universities currently using the Common Application. Every one of those essays was written on one of the Common App topics, or "prompts." Even if you're planning to apply to a non-Common-App college, you should read this chapter because the odds are high that you'll be asked to write on a topic that resembles one or more of the Common App topics. Word limits on essays written for specific colleges vary from place to place. For every Common App essay, however, the maximum number of words is 650, the minimum, 250.

You'll soon see that responses to Common App prompts can easily overlap. For instance, an essay on topic #1—defining your identity—might also include material appropriate to topic #4, about a place or environment where you find perfect contentment. Or an essay on topic #2—experiencing failure, could easily incorporate a discussion of how a particular mistake or misjudgment marked a turning point between childhood and adulthood (topic #5).

Topic #1: The "Identity" Question

Some students have a background or story that is so central to their identity that they believe their application would be incomplete without it. If this sounds like you, then please share your story.

So you haven't ridden your bike across the country, performed on *American Idol*, or won a lottery. Nor have you earned dozens of gymnastics awards or overcome the hardships of growing up homeless. In other words, you've lived a pretty ordinary life and feel as though you don't have an identity that significantly sets you apart from most other people your age. If that describes you, take heart, because it's still possible to write a winning essay that clearly defines your identity, even though you've never made headlines.

Here's why: The term *identity* has a multitude of meanings that range from the most general (*living creature, human being, male/female*) to the very specific (*volunteer in your school's chemistry lab, Lauren's older sister, over-the-top fan of horror movies*). Your identity can be a label thrust upon you by others or a trait that's personal and private. Whatever you feel, think, or do helps to define you—that is, gives you an identity. An identity can be developed, say, by the clothes you wear, the way you speak, or how you spend your time. If you are tall, good-looking, and have red hair . . . well, that's an identity. If you daydream, pray, talk, tweet, or tinker with motors a lot—those, too, are all identities.

In responding to the identity question, then, your job is to name a characteristic that defines you. In your essay, you can describe how you got that way, how it manifests itself, or more generally, why it is significant to you.

In the essay that follows, for example, Mart R tells a story meant to illustrate a trait he's proud of—a reluctance to judge other people too hastily.

I train and swim with some of my school's roughest customers. I enjoy listening to their foul-mouthed banter, their bravado, and their contempt for the rules. At swim meets they tell guys about to compete in the next lane, "If you win this

race, I'll beat the crap out of you." They have an unquench-
able appetite for violence and talk endlessly about fights—the
bloodier the better—and about guns and slutty girls. I can
contribute nothing to their conversation, so I usually keep my
mouth shut, content to observe my teammates from a
distance.

Big B is the most outwardly intimidating among them.
A natural leader, he is huge, hairy, looks like a forty-
something—older than our coach—and never loses a race.
Like a Godfather he attracts loyal followers. A swarm of guys
and girls trail behind him wherever he goes. Not long ago he
started a brawl in the cafeteria and was almost suspended.
Soon afterwards, while we were going to a swim meet on the
school bus, he casually told me, "If I didn't make trouble, I'd
lose face. My buddies—they count on me to be tough. It
makes them feel secure."

I don't know what led up to that confidence, but afterwards Big B probably regretted revealing a sensitive side of his
personality to me. He's never again spoken to me in a manner
that resembles human interaction. We nod at each other
across the locker room and grunt to each other at poolside,
but we've never talked together or ridden side-by-side to a
swim meet. Yet, in that moment of Big B's self-revelation, I
realized that he, if not all his followers, was not a total brute
but just another boy posing behind a tough mask. He's not a
wussie, but he is less barbaric than he appears and less callous
than he lets on. And ever since then I've been less apt to
make snap judgments about people, a quality that I think has
made me an all-around more tolerant person.

In responding to the so-called "identity question," be aware of
the following do's and don'ts:

DO . . .

- ✓ Write an essay that directly addresses the prompt.
- ✓ Write about your background or tell a story that is truly
  crucial to your identity.
- ✓ Be sure to define your identity fully and explicitly.
- ✓ Discuss how your story or background helps to define
  who you are today.

✓ Explain why your college application would be incomplete without a discussion of your identity.

DON'T . . .

✗ Devote the entire essay to telling a story or describing the details of your background. Leave room to discuss and define your identity.

✗ Hesitate to create interest by using dialogue and other story-writing techniques in your essay.

✗ Define yourself negatively. Colleges look for strengths rather than weaknesses. Besides, they don't need to know *everything* about you.

✗ Overstate your identity. For example, don't present yourself as a saint or a hero.

Excerpts from Answers That Worked

KINCAID R

Picking a quotation to put under my yearbook picture has been one of the hardest but ultimately most satisfying experiences I had in high school. I searched for a quote to represent my identity fully and truthfully, and in the process I rejected hundreds of sayings, lines from famous poems, song lyrics, slogans, and proverbs. Most of them seemed like recycled cheese, or too sappy or ill-fitting. When I finally narrowed my choices to ten, that's when the fun began. I had to analyze each quote in light of my concept of myself, and as I studied each one I began to understand who I am, who I am not, who I pretended to be but never could be, and who I aspire to become. That is to say, I examined myself more closely and thoughtfully than ever before and came to an eye-opening conclusion. . . .

By now, I'll bet you're dying to know which quotation I finally chose but I'm reluctant to tell you. I want to be accepted in college based not on what I think of myself but on what you think of my record, my achievements, and my potential to be an asset to your institution.

MORGAN J

The timing was perfect. I had just switched from violin to viola, an instrument I was excited about, and so my mind was open to change. For a reason I can't remember, on that spring morning my English teacher played a recording of the "Ode to Joy" from Beethoven's Ninth Symphony to the class. I knew it, of course, and could pluck out the melody on the piano, but on this day in English class I basically listened to the piece for the first time in my life.

. . . The music didn't float over my ears as classical music usually did. It came right at me. It barged into my life like a tsunami. Its spell stayed with me and gave me an outlook on classical music that has never left me. That morning in English class I was turned into a musician.

. . . Since that encounter with the "Ninth" I've become obsessed with having others share the experience of having classical music possess them. I have started preparing a program with a friend which we call "Classical is Cool," meant to teach elementary school kids about this music.

. . . I am convinced that discussing such pieces as the "Ninth," Dvorak's "American" String Quartet, and Tchaikovsky's Violin Concerto with kids, talking about how the music makes them feel, what images, or even just colors, it evokes, will show them that classical music is much more than background noise. Rather, like nothing else, the music of Bach and Brahms can be a transforming experience.

CHITA A

My mother has been the single most influential person in giving me an identity. She brought me to the United States from Puerto Rico soon after she and my father were divorced. She taught me English as a second language, but she also taught me never to forget where I came from. My mother did everything to make sure I stuck to my roots.

She enrolled me in a bilingual school and cooked only Puerto Rican dishes. She spoke to me only in Spanish. Not only did I learn to dance salsa, I developed a great sense of pride to be part of Puerto Rican culture.

. . . Sometimes it is very hard to be proud of your background if you are a minority in the United States. Wherever I go, people suspect me of being an illegal alien. Due to the huge amount of discrimination toward non-whites, I sometimes feel discouraged and wonder how I can possibly contribute to the world. But then I look at my mother and see what is possible. She is an extremely successful attorney who just happens to be Puerto Rican. Because of her example, I am confident that by having faith in my heritage and in myself, I can accomplish anything.

MARNI G

When I was very young my mother introduced me to the world of the printed page, a world as crucial to my existence as breathing. She smothered me with tales of Dr. Seuss and the adventures of Strawberry Shortcake. My dreams were filled with colorful, exciting sagas that my subconscious recreated from bedtime stories.

After a while, I became frustrated with my dependence on my mother for entrance into fantasy land. I wanted to give myself this pleasure, to own these words. My brain strived to make sense of the masses of letters so I could read by myself. Before long, I conquered this barrier, one that had kept me from experiencing this primary form of pure bliss that was known to me at this point in life. I had achieved the extraordinary—I could read. . . .

I am no longer able to devote every spare moment to consuming an endless supply of wonderful books. Yet, literature has become my secret addiction. I steal time from such urgent matters like writing term papers and prepping for exams and rendezvous briefly with authors like Shakespeare,

Jane Austen, and Ayn Rand. During moments of an increasingly busy schedule I indulge in just two or three pages of my obsession at a time. Although I've become accustomed to soaking up small doses of heavenly passion, in the back of my mind I still long for the uncomplicated world in which the Cat in the Hat is the ruler and Green Eggs and Ham the official meal.

NEWT F

"Do you have any siblings?" someone asked.

"Yes, I have one," I replied, "a brother."

"How old?"

"Twenty."

"What college does he go to?"

"Um, he's not in college. He's retarded, um, and he goes to high school with me."

"Oh, I see."

I've had conversations like this hundreds of times. Yet each one brews new emotions. Sometimes I'm proud to have a retarded brother. At other times, I'm embarrassed and feel I've been given a raw deal. "Why me?" I ask myself. Why is Kevin older than me, yet I am his big brother? Why isn't he taking me to a party at his college instead of my walking him to the bus every morning because he's scared of the neighbor's dog? . . .

Then I turn my thoughts around and realize what a huge part of my life Kevin is, and how he has changed me as a person. He has made me more caring than the average male teen, and I am more open and aware of others' emotions. . . .

I can do so many things that he can't. This is hard because he is envious of me. Whether I'm running out to a club meeting, playing soccer, rushing to band practice or play rehearsal at school, or just going out with friends, I will pause, and during that pause a guilty feeling comes over me. I can't blame him for it, but it's tinged slightly with regret, or is it resentment? Before his twentieth birthday party, he asked if some of my friends would come. I knew they wouldn't, but I could not disappoint him. "Maybe next year," I said. . . .

I try to soothe his envy of me by suggesting we do things together and choosing something that he can do. Bowling, for one. We go often to the local alley where he is known as "Big Kev." The other day after a game he said sadly, "I didn't do too good today." I put my arm over his shoulder and in a half whisper replied with words I try to live by: "You did your best. You'll get 'em next time, Kev, you'll get 'em next time." Deep inside I know this may not be true. But because there will be hundreds of games in the future, hundreds of afternoons spent together, hundreds of times when his ball might, just might roll down the middle of the alley and knock down every pin. I look forward to each and every one of them.

Topic #2: The "Failure" Question

Recount an incident or time when you experienced failure. How did it affect you, and what lessons did you learn?

Because no one passes through life without messing up or stumbling once in a while, colleges want to know how you cope with a lack of success and whether you learn from your mistakes. What you write in response to this question sheds light not only on your personality but on your overall emotional resilience.

Your essay can deal with any failure at all, from a simple *faux pas* like calling someone by the wrong name to a life-altering disaster, such as causing a fatality by driving too fast. Most application essays about failure, however, fall somewhere between such extremes. The possibilities abound: the time you botched an important exam or came too late to an appointment, an incident when you hurt someone's feelings, or told an outrageous lie, or shoplifted, or let down a friend . . . and so on.

A failure you recount in an essay ought to involve making a bad choice and then suffering consequences, anything, say, from red-faced embarrassment to out-and-out punishment. Avoid describing a failure for which you weren't responsible, as, for instance, the time you slipped on the outfield grass and thereby failed to catch the fly ball. Yes, your failure may have caused your team to lose the game, but an essay about an error made through no fault of your own won't be as insightful or compelling as one that tells of a purposeful act with disagreeable repercussions.

Writing about a personal blunder offers you a chance to convince college admissions officials that you know how to learn or benefit from a setback. Kevin R, for instance, recalled a failure involving his late grandmother. "She wasn't much fun," Kevin wrote. "Preferring to hang out with friends or go to a movie, I invented stomach aches, homework, and 'prior commitments' to avoid seeing her." After his grandmother died, Kevin realized too late that he'd squandered a once-in-a-lifetime opportunity to learn about his Irish ancestry. Saddened by ill-chosen priorities, he concluded insightfully, "I am more apt now to take the long view and see value in postponing immediate gratification."

No account of a failure is necessarily off limits in an application essay, but you should probably avoid disclosing highly personal or devastating experiences. One applicant to Stanford, for example, equated failure with date rape. She described her horrific experience in vivid, even graphic, terms. The admissions committee was stunned, but they thought the essay crossed the line of good taste, and the applicant was wait-listed.

DO . . .

- ✓ Focus on one episode, one time, or one series of similar failures.
- ✓ Pick a failure that had a direct and important effect on you.
- ✓ Explain what you learned from your failure or how it changed you.
- ✓ Discuss how changes brought about by your failure reflect on who you are today.

DON'T . . .

- ✗ Choose a trite or frivolous incident or time when something went wrong.
- ✗ Pick a failure or mistake over which you had no control.

✗ Use your essay to vent, whine, or make excuses for your lack of success or personal shortcomings.

✗ Choose a failure from long ago unless its aftereffects are still relevant.

Excerpts from Answers That Worked

FLOYD G

Late in my freshman year the student government sponsored a forum on the issue of self-segregation among black and white students in my school. It came about because of an article in the school newspaper about the fact that there are just a handful of black students in AP courses and that they have little to do with the vast majority of other black students, who are segregated in remedial classes. The article also pointed out a condition that everyone knows about but rarely talks about, that being how blacks and whites have taken over certain corners of the school as their turf. Walking through the hallways, it's easy to see which areas are "black" and which are "white." There are no official rules about which area belongs to which group. But many kids I know won't frequent certain areas because of fear of intruding.

The forum was attended mostly by whites and a few blacks. I went but said nothing. Most speakers advocated breaking down barriers between the races. As a solution, the administration proposed having a school-wide assembly on the issue in September. Everyone left hoping that interracial harmony was just over the horizon at BHS.

In my sophomore year nothing was said about the proposed assembly. The school was more concerned with students parking illegally in the teachers' parking lot. I was tempted to ask the principal about the assembly but never got around to it.

... The next year the school's main issue was widespread cheating and plagiarism on tests and papers. Every day, however, I was reminded of the racial divide in the school, especially in "C" corridor, where the black kids always gathered before and after school and lunchtime. Again, I thought about it but held my tongue.

Now, as a senior, I'm mostly occupied with applying to college. In the last two years no one in authority has brought up the racial situation in the school. No one has tried to integrate the blacks and whites. The two groups seem to have decided to maintain the status quo. I'm disheartened because schools reflect society, and if a school doesn't think it worthwhile to remedy the situation among young people, the problem of self-segregation will never go away. In a way, I blame myself for keeping silent. I failed to speak up and raise an issue that I have thought a lot about and was aware of all through high school. I feel kind of guilty, but I have made a resolution to start speaking up whenever I see a social problem that should be solved. I only hope that I have the will to follow through in college, a new stage in my life.

LIN Y

Soon after moving to California in 2011, I learned an important lesson the hard way. I learned that the old saying "What you don't know can't hurt you" is totally false.

. . . My little sister Lucy and I came home one afternoon and found a big snake on our front doormat. I was shocked and a little bit scared. Because it had no rattles, I knew it wasn't a rattlesnake, but I couldn't tell if it was another kind of poisonous snake.

. . . I decided right away that it had to go. I didn't like the idea of a snake living in our front yard and scaring us every time we went outside, especially as it hardly moved when I shouted "Scat, you snake" and shrieked other similar sounding commands. . . . Finally, because the snake seemed to have an attitude that the doormat belonged to him, I told Lucy to run to the garage and bring me a shovel. I was going to murder the creature in cold blood.

. . . Later, after my father informed me I had put to death a gopher snake, I grew terribly upset and angry with myself. As he explained, gopher snakes are not just harmless, they are the opposite because they especially like to eat gophers. . . . The stupidity of my impulsive act became evident a few weeks later when the first of several gopher mounds appeared in our front yard. By that time, I had learned that "What you don't know *can* hurt you." I also started to learn about snakes and other creatures found in the Bay Area, such as coyotes, mountain lions, owls, lizards, and hundreds of birds. I now have an iPad app to identify wildlife. I hope it will keep me from becoming a serial killer in the future.

EMMA E

I know it's impossible, but sometimes I would like to reverse my life and do things differently. If I mess up on a test or say something mean or stupid, I can't change it or get a second chance. To think otherwise would be self-delusion or an acute case of wishful thinking.

When I was about 8 years old the fantasy of doing it over became a brief reality, so brief that it lasted only about two hours on the afternoon of my birthday party.

. . .We were playing musical chairs, a game I loved. I "got out" on the third or fourth round and should have sat down next to the other girls who had been caught earlier without a chair when the music stopped. To my own surprise, I erupted into tears, insisting that because it was my birthday I deserved another chance. Of course, my demand was met. The round was re-played and this time I found a seat. . . . Eventually, I won the game. . . . I couldn't have put it into words back then but I recall feeling somewhat guilty—or a better word might be "soiled," because my victory wasn't earned. It was handed to me as a result of behaving like a spoiled brat.

. . . Almost ten years and many birthday parties later, I still feel haunted by the fact that just because I made a fuss, I was given my way. I've outgrown the guilt by now and have developed a sort of fatalistic acceptance of defeat as a natural part of life. I won't win every battle or come out on top in everything I do, but I've learned to accept failure graciously.

I probably won't be accepted at every college I apply to. I won't be devastated by rejection. . . . When an acceptance comes, however, I'll think I got admitted fairly and squarely, and that will make me super happy.

HEATHER W

. . . Miss B is the physical education teacher at my elementary school. Unfortunately, this sentence is written in the present tense, for at this very moment she is probably eroding the psyches of hundreds of children aged five through twelve. Perhaps you are thinking the word "erode" is too drastic. Well, before you accuse me of exaggeration and pretense, let me assure you that there are not enough harsh words in the English language that can sufficiently describe this woman. Fortunately, her influence on me was not completely negative. In a way, it can be regarded as a two-fold influence which finally, after many years, resulted in giving me a stronger self image. Oddly, her negative effect has allowed my determination to develop.

. . . I am sure that many people have fond memories of gym class. Those who do obviously never encountered Miss B.

The smells of gyms, the orange mats, and even the outdoor concrete on which I would occasionally slip, stimulate sickening feelings of terror and dread. . . . Miss B had a way of singling out one person and teasing him, usually the one who came in last in the broad jump or dropped the baton at the critical moment of the relay race. That was usually me. It wouldn't have been nearly so traumatic if she'd pulled me aside and scolded me for my inability to do a one-handed cartwheel. But she knew what would hurt the most. She would call an activity to a halt in order to point to the clumsy person who was doing things "wrong."

. . . As time passed, I came to realize that I would never succeed if I held her image of me to be true.

Fortunately, I was able to transform her negative influence into a goad for self-worth. . . . Her influence inspired me to show myself and others that I am not a clumsy, ineffectual person. I have become a tennis player—a rather graceful one I might add—and a skier, and a highly coordinated pianist. The more I recall her degradation of me, the more determined I have become to be courageous, confident, and perhaps even lithe. I wish I could now show her how strong I have become, not to please her or win her respect. I doubt it would work, but it would be great if she knew that because of her, I am an accomplished achiever who refused to yield to her negative influence.

Topic #3: The "Challenge" Question

Reflect on a time when you challenged a belief or idea. What prompted you to act? Would you make the same decision again?

Why would a college care whether you've ever challenged a belief or idea? You probably know the answer: A student likely to challenge beliefs and ideas generates intellectual excitement in classrooms, labs, dorms, dining halls, the library—wherever students gather. The college years are meant for expanding minds, and what activates brainwork more strikingly than controversy over long held assumptions and opinions?

The success of an essay on this topic depends partly on the nature of the challenge and how you implemented it. An account of a serious challenge carries more weight than an anecdote about a trivial one. Explain what moved you to challenge a particular idea or belief. If the issue aroused your passions, say so, but avoid presenting yourself as a militant firebrand, poised to challenge ideas and beliefs just for the thrill of creating a stir. Dissent and nonconformity are welcome on most college campuses, but not brash radicalism. Let your essay reveal your rationality and insightfulness. Show that you can be open minded and respectful of others' views, even when you don't agree with them. Such qualities of mind and heart are bound to make you welcome on any college campus.

In your essay, be sure to describe the circumstances that led you to challenge an idea or belief. During an English class discussion, for example, you may have challenged the teacher's or another student's interpretation of a poem or story. Perhaps you wrote a letter to the school newspaper objecting to rules governing computer use in the library. Maybe you spoke up at a board of education meeting or posted a blog that challenged the decision to hire an armed security guard for your school. An essay by Patty S, a senior who characterized herself as "normally a shy wallflower," told about screwing up her courage and denouncing the "antiquated criteria" for admitting new members to her school's honor society. Among other things, she recruited allies among her classmates, circulated a petition, and set up a meeting with the administration to present her case. Patty's effort turned out to be futile, but she is proud to have tried. Would she do it again? "You bet I would!" she wrote.

Non-school life also offers abundant opportunities to challenge ideas and beliefs. Perhaps you yourself have questioned some of your family's entrenched rules, routines, and beliefs. At seventeen, virtually an adult, should you, like a child half your age, still be required to eat everything on your plate? What about the parental curbs on your TV watching until homework is done or the imperative to call or text if you're going to arrive home more than fifteen minutes late?

Today's headline issues, from gay marriage to global warming, are also subject to challenges. Every year admissions officials can count on stacks of essays from students who have attended rallies, solicited funds, or in some other way have challenged the status quo. A significant number of essays have recently come from applicants supporting a ban on the use of plastic grocery bags in their communities. Students in other places have described their efforts to overturn such bans.

A challenge to an idea or belief need not take place in public. Most people, but especially the young, live in a state of flux, quietly puzzling out the validity of what they've been told or taught since birth. In the privacy of their own minds they grapple with issues of morality, human rights, religion, happiness, death, love, and much, much more. Perhaps you've pondered such matters, too, and found yourself having second—or even third and fourth—thoughts about your very own core beliefs and values. If so, you have an application essay waiting to be written. Go for it!

DO . . .

- ✓ Respond to all three parts of the prompt but not necessarily in equal proportions.
- ✓ State the reasons why you challenged a particular idea or belief.

✓ Explain the circumstances and the manner in which you challenged an idea or belief.

✓ Describe the most important effects of your challenge, both good and bad.

DON'T . . .

✗ Reject writing about a challenge that didn't work out as you had hoped or expected.

✗ Devote your essay primarily to argue against the idea or belief you challenged.

✗ Adopt a self-righteous or superior tone, as if to say that the idea or belief you have challenged is obviously stupid or misguided.

✗ Use the essay to attack, mock, or insult those whose idea or belief you challenged.

Excerpts from Answers That Worked

CHARLYN H

As part of my school's community service requirement I chose to be a "friendly visitor" to residents in the local nursing home. Everyone told me, "You're going to regret it. It's so depressing."

I went anyway, hoping they were mistaken. They weren't. It was totally depressing, but I never regretted it. Many residents were glued to daytime television, rarely leaving their rooms. Some sat lined up in corridors dazed or drugged and slumped in wheelchairs. They appeared disconnected from the world and usually seemed not to care about having a visitor, friendly or not.

Everyone thought I was wasting my time sitting with senile, despairing people, reading the newspaper to them or trying to converse with them. At times I agreed.

Even so, I kept thinking and hoping that maybe I was somehow getting through to them. At times, their eyes flashed as if they understood what I was saying, or they nodded their heads or answered my questions appropriately. Occasionally, they said something related to an article in the news that I had read aloud to them.

. . . My optimism was rewarded finally when I met a ninety-six-year-old woman, Mrs. Lillian Everson. The supervisor warned me that since she was almost blind and deaf, communication with her would be quite difficult. On the first day I took the newspaper with me. If all conversation failed, I could at least try to read to her.

Within a few minutes, the tension of our first meeting was gone. Although Mrs. Everson was hard of hearing, if I spoke directly to her, she could understand me by reading my lips. Soon, we actually began to tell each other about our families and past histories. I went home that day feeling triumphant, still holding the unopened newspaper in my hands.

In spite of what I'd been told, Mrs. Everson soon stopped being an old woman in my mind. She became a friend who relied on me and appreciated me because I respected her and recognized her dignity. I still visit her. Some weeks she is more vibrant than others. Even on her bad days I see an intelligence and courage that inspire me. . . . She reminds me that growing old is not always a desperate process, where all pride and hope are lost.

KAREN R

SHOCKED! That is what I was while reading a book called *The Other America* by Michael Harrington for my American history class.

The book opened my eyes to what Harrington called "the cycle of poverty and hopelessness" of millions of Americans who are stuck in dismal poverty generation after generation. The author says that poor people are basically hidden from view, and are hardly helped at all by all the anti-poverty and social programs meant to lift them up . . .

Being convinced that their condition is a permanent part of American life and that nothing could be done about it, I was very skeptical of an announcement I saw tacked to my church bulletin board that said, "Volunteers Wanted." The fine print said that poor people in the town of D———, New York had been given notice of eviction from their houses, which had been condemned by the government as "unfit for human habitation." Volunteers were needed to go upstate and help fix up the existing housing to prevent the displacement of dozens of families.

. . . When we arrived in D——— I couldn't believe the poverty of the people and the enormity of the job. Besides being hot, unbearably hot, the town was disgustingly dirty and run down. A scrawny dog barked at me. Barefoot children stood in the dust and stared at me with sad vacant eyes as I wondered what on earth I was doing there while all my friends were hedonistically shagging rays at the beach back home and having fun.

. . . Hopelessness surrounded me, yet my minister's hope could never be dashed. He smiled and urged us on. "Let's do it," he said. "Let's save these houses from the dozer." His spirit made me feel ashamed of my pessimism, so I pitched in with all my might to clean up the squalid, rat- and cockroach-infested shacks.

. . . During six weeks of intensive labor I saw some progress made with my own hands. I left a tiny corner of the world in better shape than when I found it. I will continue my campaign to help my fellow man. I hope to join the Peace Corps after college. Wherever they send me I'll go with a much greater hope and a greater understanding of mankind and myself.

KRISTIN G

Last year, when my grandfather had a stroke and was dying of cancer in the hospital, my parents decided to remove life support to let him die peacefully and end his suffering. I was horrified by their decision and I let them know it. I protested, cried, yelled at them, and called them "beasts," "monsters," and "murderers." They were shattered by my reaction to their very difficult decision. For days, as life ebbed from my grandfather's body, my parents and I barely spoke to each other.

Then Maggie, a nurse in the hospital, gave me an essay by Sidney Hook after I talked with her about my grandfather. The essay "In Defense of Voluntary Euthanasia" supports a pro-euthanasia opinion. At one point in his life, Hook had a near-death experience and includes it in his essay, giving the essay a realistic and personal effect. "I have already paid my dues to death—indeed, although time has softened my memories they are vivid enough to justify my saying that I suffered enough to warrant dying several times over. Why run the risk of more?" Hook felt like he had his fill of happiness in life and therefore he had no need to prolong it. In addition, he felt that procedures that are used to prolong lives but don't lead to recovery are terrible and costly inconveniences to the patient's family members.

I'm glad Maggie showed me the essay. It changed my mind. It made the terrible decision more acceptable to me. At the same time, however, I regretted giving my parents such a hard time. I made the ordeal they were going through so much worse for them. It was thoughtless of me to speak out. I was so wrapped up in my own feelings that I could not understand theirs. When I should have been supportive, I was exactly the opposite. I'm still remorseful and sad.

AILEEN S

Last summer I took a job as a counselor at Apple Pines, a residential camp for children with emotional and behavioral problems. On the very first day, one of my campers, Cassius, spit at me because I told him he couldn't spit at other kids. Then he fell on the grass, screamed profanities, and threw rocks.

The other counselors were all high school and college kids, not really experienced in caring for the types of kids at Apple Pines. To help us do our jobs, the camp director held regular training meetings which often turned into gripe sessions where counselors complained and sometimes even wept about the difficulty of the work and their inability to cope with kids they nicknamed "Rotten Robbie," "Diego the Dreadful" and other pejoratives not appropriate in a college application essay. Almost half the counselors, frustrated and desperate, quit their jobs at the place they called Apple Pines Asylum within a few weeks.

I stayed on, thinking it wasn't as bad as all that. In a week or two I had become inured to bed-wetting and spitting and had learned to shrug off kids' derogatory comments about my mother. I had begun to see the endearing personalities that children like Cassius possess. At the training meetings and even informally, I spoke up in favor of the kids and made observations about many good things that were happening around the camp. I was called "Pollyanna" and "Rosie" because of my rose-colored glasses.

All summer, I crusaded on behalf of Cassius, a crack baby with cerebral palsy and ADHD. His hyperactivity was astounding, and his inappropriate behavior was ceaseless. Countless times I watched the smallest incident drive Cassius into a spitting, cursing fit of hysteria. Yet beneath his tantrums was an adorable boy seeking love and attention.

. . . When camp ended, I was completely unprepared to leave Cassius. I couldn't face sending him back to his myriad of foster mothers and multitudes of schools. Camp showed Cassius consistency, and with it, his behavior improved. Temper tantrums became less frequent, and spitting was reduced to a reaction to anger rather than an attention-getting scheme. Leaving camp, I cried for all my campers, sad that they had to go back to families that neglected or abused them, but happy that each of them had enjoyed camp.

. . . Getting on the bus, Cassius whispered to me, "Will you play with me forever?" I smiled regretfully and said, "I wish I could, Cassius. I wish I could."

. . . Cassius's birthday was yesterday. I called but couldn't speak to him because he was away for the weekend with his birth mother. . . . I think about him a lot and hope there are other people in the world who are ready to love Cassius as I do and to remind him of the success he could achieve.

Topic #4. The "Setting" Question

Describe a place or environment where you are perfectly content. What do you do or experience there, and why is it meaningful to you?

If you are lucky enough to have a favorite spot where you feel happy, fulfilled, and perfectly content, this topic may be for you. If you're really lucky, you'll have several such retreats from everyday cares.

The phrase "place or environment," however, has a multitude of meanings, and, therefore, can be literally anywhere: your bed, the beach, a mountaintop, the local pizzeria. Just as easily, it could be somewhere not found on a map. You might feel fully at peace, for instance, while perusing Facebook, partying with friends, helping your kid brother with his homework, viewing the stars on a clear night. While not literally "a place or environment," a state of mind can also beget contentment. Take, for example, a sense of personal accomplishment, or moments when you are so deeply sunk into work or play that all your worldly cares and concerns virtually disappear. Many people find contentment while daydreaming or allowing their minds to wander aimlessly. Emotional states also breed contentment: feeling at home, being in love, enjoying nature's beauty . . . the list goes on and on. Likewise, the past and future are also "places," as is the world of imagination and fantasy.

An essay on this topic should identify the setting where you feel content. It should also contain an account of what happens to you in that place, emotionally, physically, or in any other way. Obviously, you feel good while being there, but don't be satisfied to leave it at that. Instead, dig deeper. Seek the specific reasons you feel that way. Show detailed evidence of your contentment in terms of what you say and think and do.

Scottie V, for instance, whose contentment derives from running long distances, described his feelings this way:

The ability to push through the sea of lactic acid that lies between one step and the next requires an immense amount of mental determination. At the end of the run, when my shoes are unlaced and the spandex is thrown into the laundry,

> I've not only grown physically and mentally stronger, I've enjoyed myself and know that I've used my day well.

In her response to this question, high school senior Annie A picked "anywhere that's risky" as the place where she feels most content. She then uses a brief anecdote to convey her reaction to being caught by an incoming tide on a remote Pacific beach:

> The roaring waves slammed with tremendous force against the rock, making it extremely difficult to hold on. I realized that I could die here, but as usual, I assumed that I would be O.K. Surprisingly, I was overcome by a sense of calm. . . .
>
> Too many people in the world define "impossible" as *not capable of existing or happening*. They say to themselves, "It cannot be done." I look at things differently. When I hear "impossible," my mind translates this to *tough*, and maybe even *extremely difficult to deal with*. Difficult, sure, but never insurmountable, never impossible. Other people find it hard to believe, but when I face danger, I'm overcome with a kind of heavenly contentment.

DO . . .

✓ Pick a place or environment you know well, not one you've been to only once or twice.

✓ Consider what your choice of place says about you.

✓ Focus your essay not on the location but on its affects on you.

✓ Highlight one or two significant affects rather than several minor ones.

DON'T . . .

✗ Necessarily limit your choice of place to a specific geographical location.

✗ Pick a place where your contentment is artificially induced by smoke or drink.

✗ Ignore the bounds of good taste in describing the place and your reaction to it.

✗ Be excessively sappy or sentimental about the place.

Excerpts from Answers That Worked

CHRIS J

Last summer I spent six weeks with my father on Moosehead Lake in Maine. When I wasn't working at Squaw Mountain Resort, I was helping my father build a house which was a little more elaborate than a typical summer home.

Our isolated piece of land is two miles from the main road and seven miles from the nearest "town." Being so far from the rushing competiveness of my usual suburban world was an illuminating experience for me. Each time I gazed at the mammoth expanse of water through the picture window of the new house, there before me was a different scene right out of a nature calendar.

Whole days would pass without a single boat passing, even in the distance. Instead, there were mournful cries of loons, and occasionally the splashing of a moose in the shallows of the lake.

I found that in between painting and hammering, much of my time was spent in complete solitude. Like Thoreau at Walden Pond, I found this solitude deeply satisfying. To get up to see the sun rise, to go for a long run, and then to bathe in the startlingly cold lake were more than refreshing. It caused me to appreciate fully the awesome qualities of Mother Nature and to feel at one with her.

Surprisingly, much as I enjoy being alone, I also relish personal relationships. I can revel in solitude or be gregarious—whatever fits the situation. . . . My time at the lake opened my eyes to the fact that I need both solitude and friends to be truly content.

CLARISSA H

(The lights dim, the theme music begins, the audience settles down.)

"I am Betty Parris. I am Betty Parris, I am . . ." Lock the audience out. Don't look at them. Concentrate inside. I am Betty Parris. What are my intentions? I want power. I want to be stronger than Abigail. Why? She can manipulate me, and she can twist my emotions to fit the intricate mind games she plays. I'm cold as ice, and I feel my nerves hardening. Slowly all my good intentions will seep away into my surroundings and I will be purely evil. There's no going back now. Murder is final. I'll sacrifice whatever or whoever I need to, but I will prevail. Now I am Betty Parris. . . .

Acting on stage is turning yourself into someone else. Performing in *The Crucible*, I realize that becoming a character means incorporating that person into who I am. I no longer played Betty Parris. As her traits became mine, her deep, dark secrets became mine, too. I became another person.

By taking on the identity of Betty I dug into myself, dredged up my worst points, and magnified them in order to make my performance effective. On the stage, Betty's teeth were clenched, her hands balled into fists. Her shoulders almost shook from the strain. Her bodily movements became more forceful, as though each action was full of the desire to lash out at the other actors, especially the girl playing Abigail. Her anger was so profound that she wished she would die.

Meanwhile, where was Clarissa? That is to say, where was the person who used to be Clarissa? She had temporarily abandoned her body, mind, and spirit. All her fears, anxieties, worries, tensions, nervousness now resided in Betty, and Clarissa on the stage was more content and happier than she'd ever been before.

KATE O

I am "Aqua-Girl" (half human, half fish). Last summer I became a certified PADI Junior Open Water Diver. So far, I have completed seven dives off the California coast and fifteen dives at the Galapagos Islands during Christmas. I swam with the turtles, rays, and even a whale shark! Three years ago, when my family and I went to the Great Barrier Reef, I was too young to scuba dive, as I was under thirteen, but snorkeling on the surface, I could see the scuba divers with the giant grouper and other sea creatures. . . .

From an early age, the human side of me has loved fishing. I used to tag along with my father to the local man-made fishing pond and try to "roll-cast" with his fly-rods. The first fishing trip our family took was to Alaska. There we caught almost everything you can find in the seafood section of a supermarket. From then on, fishing rods were part of almost every family vacation. The biggest fish I ever caught was a 140-pound tarpon in Florida. Some of my other fishing adventures have included salmon fishing where the Columbia River meets the Pacific, casting for blues on Cape Cod, lobstering in the Gulf of Mexico, and trawling for fish in Australia and Malaysia.

. . . As someone who has spent most of her life near, on, or in the sea, it may strike you as odd that I'd like to go to college so far inland. But that is just the point. In college I want to be exposed to the unfamiliar, the out of the ordinary, the strange. I want to know whether endless miles of corn and soybean fields can provide as much contentment as the vastness of the ocean.

. . . and by the way, I've read *Moby Dick*—twice!

AARON L

A cool wind greets me under the hot lights as the curtain rises. I hear applause, a variety of whistles and shouts—then cheers as our drummer counts off: 1 . . . 2 . . . 3 . . . 4. Simultaneously, the four musicians come alive, all making different sounds, yet blasting it out in one mighty explosion. At first I stroke my electric guitar nervously. I think about each and every note I must hit precisely. Sweat gathers on my brow. I feel everyone is looking at me. My eyes wander. I take note that the crowd is dancing, enjoying, not critiquing. Gradually, I begin to relax. I no longer think about what I need to do, I sense it. And not only can I feel the beat, I feel affection and warmth from my band mates, who are my closest friends, and from the crowd, who, for the time we play, also become close friends. I am overcome, overjoyed with feelings of euphoria and security . . .

* * *

. . . The sign at the trailhead reads "2 miles (steep uphill)." "Dad, are you sure this is what we should do today?"

"Come on, it's a beautiful hike."

The four of us begin. Steps, inclines, rocks, roots—not my usual idea of a vacation day. Strangely, however, I find myself enjoying this excursion. Granted, the ascent is beautiful: tall trees, a running stream, birds singing, but I don't believe that this is the root of my delight. It's more the company. My sister, my mother, and my father. Just the four of us, all alone, trudging along, talking together, and simply basking in the joy of it all. It's times like these, spent with the most special of all units, the family, that gives me contentment and helps me realize exactly how fortunate I am.

Topic #5. The "Coming-of-Age" Question
Discuss an accomplishment or event, formal or informal, that marked your transition from childhood to adulthood within your culture, community, or family.

This topic is a gift. As someone going through the process, you've probably amassed a treasure trove of essay-worthy tales about leaving childhood behind. Becoming an adult by definition, means experiencing change, and because change of any kind rarely comes easily, you probably have a good deal to say about what it has been like for you.

The transition from childhood to adulthood is marked by a series of firsts: first date, first time driving a car, first paycheck from a first job, first credit card of your own, a first trip alone to a far-off place. All these events and others are fodder for application essays, but frankly, do yourself a favor. Don't be tempted to write about such conventional experiences. Essay readers in college admissions offices have heard it all before, and they may be less than thrilled to read another essay about, say, the delights of owning a driver's license with your name on it. If you can, choose a more atypical experience, and keep your essay from getting lost in a flood of others on the very same subject.

Here's another caveat: In the past, countless students have submitted essays about the ordeal of making college plans, filling out applications, writing application essays—experiences that clearly mark a transition to adulthood. But again, you'd be better off taking a less-traveled route because many essays about what admissions officials call "application blues" border on the banal. To give your application a leg up, pick an event or accomplishment that no one else is likely to have experienced in exactly the same way. Connie G, for example, composed just such an essay, excerpted here:

> Last year, my grandmother, "Ya-ya," fell and broke her hip. With no one to turn to because my parents were away on a business trip, I acted fast. I dialed 911, checked Ya-ya into the hospital, filled out all the forms, dealt with the doctors and nurses in the ER, approved the necessary surgery, and spent the night at Ya-ya's bedside. Only then did I phone my parents.
> . . . That day marks my transformation from a child to an adult. From then on, I knew that I had it in me to handle almost any difficult situation.

Connie claims that her coming-of-age was triggered by a specific incident. Most young people, however, ripen more gradually into adulthood. Their childish ways diminish by degrees. An essay about such a change might focus, for instance, on matters of interpersonal relationships. More often than not, young children are "me-firsters." That is, they act as though the world revolves around them. Over time, their egocentrism tends to fade, and they learn to put aside self-interest for the sake of others. They realize that sacrificing themselves for the well-being of a group, although sometimes painful, is the right thing to do. In short, they begin to think and act in an adult manner.

Similarly, children begin early on to distinguish right from wrong. But it takes life experience to discern subtle shades of gray in what once may have seemed like clear-cut black and white situations. Events that involve moral dilemmas, for example, can forcefully illustrate mature and perceptive thinking. A moral bind, for example, occasioned Hannah W's essay:

> My friend Hillary invited me join her and her family for a long weekend in a rented vacation house in the mountains. I accepted gladly but was startled to hear that Dana, another girl in our school, was coming, too. I didn't know that Hillary and Dana were that friendly. Actually, I thought the opposite because at least twice I had overheard Dana spreading nasty rumors and bad-mouthing Hillary behind her back.

Knowing the truth about Dana's dislike of Hillary, I loathed the prospect of being stuck with both of them for four days in the mountains. As Hillary's friend, I also felt duty-bound to tell her what Dana had said, but I didn't want to hurt her feelings. For days I worried and pondered what to do. I thought of asking my parents, but decided not to because I could almost predict what they would say. Mom would say that I had to tell Hillary, and Dad would advise me either to stay home or try to forget it and go have fun in the mountains.

Hanna goes on to explain that she declined to inform Hillary. Instead, thinking that Dana should be held accountable for being two-faced, she confronted Dana and asked why she would accept an invitation from someone she despised. Dana denied the accusation but soon told Hillary that she couldn't go away for the weekend after all.

Later, when Hannah told her parents what she'd done, both lauded her for handling the situation so discreetly. At the same time, however, she frets about keeping Hillary in the dark, and wondering, "Am I morally obligated to tell my friend the truth?"

DO . . .

✓ Choose an event or accomplishment not likely to be chosen by other applicants.

✓ Identify a specific event or an achievement that attests meaningfully to your coming-of-age as an adult.

✓ Include details about how the event or accomplishment changed you.

✓ Create interest by dramatizing events using dialogue or other story-telling techniques.

DON'T . . .

✗ Pick this topic unless you've thought carefully how an event or accomplishment made a real difference in your life.

✗ Choose an accomplishment solely to impress your readers.

✗ Pick an accomplishment you've discussed in another part of your application.

✗ Explain too much. Let the story of the event or accomplishment speak for itself.

Excerpts from Answers That Worked

MICHAEL M

"How in the world do you know where anything is in this room, with all this junk?" said my mother one night while I was doing math homework. Putting my books aside, I began to think: "Yeah, I'll be in college next year and should start acting more like an adult. I should get rid of things I've outgrown."

The next day I started the winnowing process, trying to locate things I didn't want or need anymore. I found everything I ever saved from childhood—G.I. Joe action figures in a box, big cartons of Legos, used when I dreamed of becoming an architect; then, I happened upon transformers for toy robots, my Cub Scout manual. . . . Finally, I came to a small cigar box labeled PRIVATE. I knew immediately what was inside, but I had to make sure everything was safe. Stuffed into the box were an old silver coin that commemorated Lincoln's birthday, a two dollar bill, and a small bible. The bible was falling apart. Inside its cover, under my grandmother's name, was printed in large block letters the name JAMES, my father. It had been my father's bible when he was a boy. After my grandmother died, it was given to me. Inside in a clear baggie tucked into "Deuteronomy" was a pressed flower from Granny's funeral. This was the most cherished thing I owned. It wasn't a gift bought at the local toy store; it was a precious part of my life as well as part of my grandmother's and father's lives. They are things that I would never get rid of—never!

. . . And when my mother asks me again, which she inevitably will, to get rid of my junk, I will plainly tell her, "This isn't junk, this is my life."

DREW G

Last summer I ran headlong into a change in my life. Until then, I didn't think much about what would become of me. I simply assumed that I'd go to college, get a job, get married, have kids, and live happily every after in a pleasant suburban town such as my own. How this fantasy would come to pass I hadn't a clue. I didn't think about it. Like everything else it my life, I just assumed it would just happen naturally if I continued going to school, did my homework, said no to drugs, and went to church. Somehow I took it for granted that a good life would be provided.

Seventeen years of being shielded from reality were shattered on my first morning as a caddy at the local country club. While waiting for my assignment, I began to eavesdrop on the conversations in the caddy yard. One of my fellow caddies told of how he got drunk last night and began a bar brawl. Another told of trying to cash a welfare check that he had found in the street. Still another described how he struggled to keep his family going on food stamps and tips from caddying. I was startled, not because of their style of living, but that these grown men had no dreams, no goal in life to work toward. They seemed content to collect handouts from the government and to work at a dead-end job carrying the golf bags for club members. . . . They lived day by day and never thought of tomorrow.

. . . Suddenly I saw myself twenty years from now sitting in the caddy yard exchanging anecdotes with others just like them, and was struck dumb with worry. I couldn't live like them. The monotony of it would kill me before the alcohol would. I began to see school as more than just homework and tests without purpose, but as a way to improve myself. I found within me a drive and determination I had not known existed. I resolved to do better. I wasn't a kid anymore. I realized that going to college was more than something to do for four years. It was a necessity, an invaluable tool that would help me to magnify my determination to make something of myself and use my new-found ambition.

MIKE B

In second grade I was diagnosed as having a seizure disorder that has diminished through high school but nevertheless remains a constant threat.

. . . Although having epileptic seizures is dreadful, they have become valuable to me because I learned a lot and in many ways have became a stronger person. I haven't enjoyed the years in which epilepsy has been part of my life, but I appreciate their value and have grown proud of the way I learned to conduct myself. I stayed strong academically and came to realize just how important my education is. The fact that I was able to excel academically during a period of time which was really very hard has built up my confidence. I came to understand that being educated was one of the values I considered most important, especially being educated about the epileptic seizures that were shaping my life.

Most important was that I made up my mind to cure myself of epilepsy by becoming more informed about it. I really couldn't cure the disease itself but I could learn to live with it by understanding all there is to know. With the commitment of a professional researcher, I have spent countless hours online reading descriptions of other epileptics and their problems. I sent questions to doctors and other experts in the field. Assisted by the Epilepsy Research Foundation, I set up a web page and placed appeals on Craig's List, through which I was able to raise funds. Twice in high school, I exceeded my goal of $1000 per year. By sharing my experiences with other epileptics I made friends and found ways of dealing with it.

. . . In the beginning I wouldn't talk about my problem and even forbade my parents to mention that it existed. I was embarrassed and ashamed. But now I am more open socially and have learned to communicate with and trust my friends. Epilepsy is no longer a stigma; it's a way of life.

CHRISTINA S

My father has given me many wonderful gifts. Because of him, I am tall, green-eyed, well-coordinated, and pretty good in school. But he also gave me something that for a long time I could have done without: a full head of bright red hair. "Why couldn't I have been born a brunette, like my sister?" I asked. Instead, I always stood out like a ripe tomato in a fresh green salad.

The reason I especially disliked my hair when I was younger was because I'd be called names like "Red" and "Reddy Foxx" and "OJ" and "Carrot Top." Many times these nicknames would stick and I would lose my identity as Christina and become "The Redhead."

. . . When I finally reached the age when I no longer wanted to be a clone of everyone else, I realized that my hair distinguished me from others. This was a turning point for me. I started to believe that I was unique, and as much as I hate to admit it, I began to relish the attention I got. . . . Now I use my red hair as the basis of my individuality. This discovery has led to a new sense of confidence. It has affected the way I see myself. I began to speak out in class and in groups instead of retiring shyly into the background. I can now speak with assurance of an adult in front of groups, enabling me to become involved more fully in school, community, and church activities. . . .

Another good thing that has come from what I considered the traumatic experiences of being teased at an early age, is that I am more aware of the feelings of others, and I often find myself defending people from being ridiculed. I now see my red hair as an important part of my personality. And if someone says, "Hey, look at that redhead," I smile and say to myself, "Hey, thanks Dad."

Supplements to the Common Application

Many Common App supplements include essay questions, some of them labeled "optional." The word *optional* means what it says: It's your call whether or not to respond. Before you decide, however, consider the following: Unless you write something preposterous, you have nothing to lose and everything to gain by submitting a piece of writing. What you say may not make a whit of difference in the admissions sweepstakes, but the fact that you've taken the trouble to write something could work in your favor. In fact, your answer might actually give your application just enough of a bounce to lift it into the "accept" pile. In other words, show the college that you're not one to take the easy way out. Answer every supplemental question, optional or not, as fully and enthusiastically as you can.

Although supplementary questions may differ in detail from one college to another, they fall loosely into the following categories: (1) Why go to college, and why here? (2) Who are you? (3) What is important to you? and (4) Is there anything else you would like to say about yourself?

In the sample questions and topics listed in the pages that follow, you may not find the exact question your college asks, but you'll probably recognize one that comes close.

Why Go to College? Why Here?

From questions about your plans for the future, colleges hope to discern your route for the next four years. What will the college experience mean to you? Will you study, or will you party? Have you thought at all about why you're going to college? Expecting you to lay out your long-term educational plans, colleges ask such questions as these:

—Why do you want to go to college?
—Why do you want to go to this college, in particular?
—What are your career objectives, and how will college help you achieve them?
—How will this college help you fulfill your goals and aspirations?
—What will your presence add to this college?

No one answer to such questions is preferable to another becaus+e no college seeks to crowd its campus with only one type of student. For the most part, colleges try to keep their enrollments balanced. They may want some students intent on headng into careers in dentistry or corporate law and others hell-bent toward journalism, teaching, the biological sciences, and other fields. If you haven't made up your mind, don't fret. At age seventeen or eighteen, it's not a weakness or a defect to admit candidly that you don't yet know how you want to spend the next sixty or seventy years of your life. College is for exploring, after all, and colleges welcome students with open minds who'll rummage through many courses and programs on which they've built their reputation.

As you describe your educational aspirations, be mindful of these essay-writing guidelines:

DO . . .

✓ Answer the question being asked, not the one you'd like to answer.

✓ Before writing a word, scrutinize the college's offerings. If you expect to major in, say, ecology, be sure the college has an environmental studies program.

✓ Think hard about what *you* hope to get out of college, avoiding clichés, such as "I want an education," "I want to get a good, well-paying job," and "I want to be a success in my chosen field."

✓ Try to figure out why this college appeals to you. Did the college representatives make it sound exciting? Did you visit the campus and fall in love with the place? Is there a particular program that attracts your interest or a professor you'd like to study with?

✓ Focus on educational or personal reasons for going to college, not on social, economic, or family reasons.

DON'T . . .

✗ Use flattery. All colleges already know how good they are.

✗ Stress that you love the college's location, size, or appearance. By applying there, you have implied that those characteristics are acceptable to you.

✗ Tell a college that it's your "safe" school.

✗ Write that you're going to college because your family expects you to.

Finally, don't take any of these precautions as the last word in application essay writing. Use them at your discretion. Don't ignore them, though, unless you have a sound reason for doing so. Jim D, for example, came right out and told Bowdoin he wanted to go there precisely because of its location. "Like Thoreau," Jim wrote, "I feel most alive near wild streams and forests."

Dow T's visit to Yale convinced him to apply. In his essay, he reinforces his commitment by referring to specific people and groups he met during a weekend visit to the campus: "From the Whiffenpoofs, who performed at my high school last year, to the activist crowd I met in Dwight Hall during my visit last April, I sense that Yale is packed with people who've 'got passion' and are 'smart with heart.' My friend, David Kim, a senior at Yale, wishes he could stay another year; his college has become his family. Mr. Luckett from the admissions office told me, 'Yale doesn't accept the smartest—only the best.' And no kidding—I want to be a member of the Purple Crayon Club."

Answers That Worked

Marian T's afterschool work in a fabric shop inspired her love of fashion and developed her flair for design. "In college," Marian wrote, "I plan to major in fine arts."

David B studied four languages in high school. Because of his bent toward languages and foreign cultures, he wants a career in international affairs as a businessman or diplomat, but he said, "A couple of years in the Peace Corps will come first."

Lisa C loves to read. "I can't imagine a career more suited to me than librarian in a school or a public library," she wrote.

Wendy W has wide and wandering interests. Last year it was dance, this year it is community service. Wendy thinks of college as a place for "accumulating more interests, for meeting people, for working hard, and, ultimately, for finding a niche in life to fill."

Andy S has always taken the hardest courses. He doesn't know why, except that doing well in tough courses has made him feel good. "I hope to continue feeling good in college," he quipped.

———————

Deena R admires one of her high school English teachers. Since he's told her wonderful stories of Williams College, she'd like to go there, too. "I plan to major in English," she wrote, "and find out if Mr. Stern's stories are true."

———————

Karen S's "most joyful and gratifying high school experience" has been working with mentally retarded children. In college she'll major in special education.

———————

Mark D lost his father and a brother last year. Yet he has retained his essential optimism. He wrote that "there is still a promise in life for me. There are so many things that I have not yet experienced, but inevitably must. That's why I want to go to college."

———————

Don Z has met many people through playing guitar at festivals and nightspots. He thrives on people whose style of living differs from his. Don asked, "What better place than a giant university is there for finding a variety of people?"

———————

Becky B is thinking of a career in acting. She expects a college education to help her become a more complete person. "My wish," she wrote, "is not only to be a good actor but also a good person, and my belief is that they might be the same thing."

———————

Who Are You?

Colleges have heard what others think of you—teachers, counselors, interviewers. With self-assessment questions, they hope to learn what you think of yourself. Do you know who you are? Are you aware of how others react to you? Would you like to change in some way? Self-knowledge is often thought to be a prerequisite for understanding the world, and an essay that demonstrates that you know yourself will give your application a big boost. To check the depth of your insight, colleges ask questions like these:

—What is important to you?
—How would you describe yourself as a human being?
—How might a freshman roommate describe you?
—Write your own recommendation to college.
—If you could strengthen one aspect of yourself, what would it be? Why?
—What quality do you like best in yourself? What quality do you like least?
—Imagine yourself as a book or other object. How would people react to you?
—What makes you different from other people?

Notice that these "who-are-you?" questions resemble the Common App's "identity" question. You might, therefore, face the prospect of writing two essays on virtually the same topic. If possible, avoid it, but if you can't, let the second essay show readers in the college admissions another side of you. In other words, make sure the content in the two essays doesn't overlap.

> Telling the truth doesn't mean you must bare your soul.

Whatever you say about yourself, tell the truth. You needn't bare your soul or disclose deep, dark secrets. Colleges don't need to know about drug and drinking experiences, your sex life, or psychiatric problems. Essays on such subjects, says Barbara-Jan Wilson, formerly the dean of admissions at Wesleyan and now a university vice president, "show poor judgment and are not relevant to admission to college." On the other hand, you needn't portray yourself as a saint or modern day Goody Two-shoes. Recognizing that no one is perfect, many applicants have written gripping but thoughtful essays about their favorite vices: cynicism, greed, envy, gluttony, and so forth. In the end, let good taste govern your choice of material. If you have doubts, switch topics. Jenny G wrote an essay about a family drug problem, thought the better of it afterward, and wrote another, highlighting her good judgment.

DO . . .

✓ Answer the question that is asked.

✓ Be as honest as you can. Search for qualities you really have, not those you wish for.

✓ Emphasize specific, observable qualities that show your distinctive personality. Imagine that your reader will someday have to pick you out in a crowd.

✓ Illustrate your qualities with specific examples. Use telling anecdotes to support your opinions of yourself.

✓ Ask people who know you well whether they agree with your self-analysis.

DON'T . . .

✗ Be evasive. Stand up for what you think about yourself.

✗ Be too cute or coy. Sincerity is preferable.

✗ Choose a characteristic merely to impress the college.

✗ Write everything you know about yourself. Focus on one or two of your outstanding qualities.

✗ Write an essay fit only for a supermarket tabloid.

Remember that you can violate every rule and still write a compelling essay. Just be aware of the perils.

Answers
That
Worked

Suzannah R thinks of herself as a dynamo in danger of burning out by age twenty. She can't control her energy level. She's impatient and often intolerant of others' laid-back attitudes. She added, "As I have grown older, I feel I am learning to accept other people's shortcomings."

David V said, "The most important fact to know about me is that I am a Black person in a White society." David considers himself an outsider and expects to continue feeling alienated as long as racial prejudice exists.

———————

Ellen E contrasted her goofing off early in high school ("personal problems and just plain stupidity") with her productive junior and senior years. In effect, she was reborn during the summer between tenth and eleventh grades.

———————

Cheryl B describes herself as having been "painfully shy" in ninth and tenth grade. Encouraged by a friend, she joined the Link Crew, a student group that helps freshmen adjust to high school. Forced to speak out and set an example, she unexpectedly found within herself qualities of leadership—a discovery that, as she she put it, was a "mind-blowing experience."

———————

Steve M sees himself as a latter-day Clarence Darrow, always standing in defense of the little guy, often taking the minority point of view in class just to generate a little controversy. If others consider him obnoxious, he claimed, "it's a small price to pay for a life full of heated debates and discussions."

———————

Adam L works 25 to 30 hours a week during the school year loading and unloading trucks for the family business. He says that working such long hours "means I don't get to 'live' as much." But he takes solace in thinking that he knows the value of hard work and when he graduates from college, he'll be better prepared for the real world.

———————

John K sees himself as a character in a movie. When he's alone he pretends he's Zac Ephron, playing the role of a Generation Y bachelor. He even hums background film music when he's driving and jogging.

———————

Brendan B is a gourmet cook. He loves to eat. "You are what you eat," he believes, so he defined himself by the food he enjoys most. From meat and potatoes, for example, he has gained a strong will. From French sauces, he has derived a subtle sense of humor.

Nicole W is a perfectionist. From schoolwork to keeping her room in order, she cannot allow herself to do anything shabbily or incomplete. She is worried about "getting a slob for a college roommate."

Dena P, a gymnast since age eight, wrote that she "works like a demon" to be number one. Ever striving for perfection, she added, "I know now that when it comes to making commitments, I can be ready to make them."

Doug M is an adopted Korean orphan. He sees himself as a child of two cultures. Although a double identity causes confusion in others, he feels "more fortunate and richer" than his American classmates.

Jocelyn B loves social networking. Everything about it comes so easily and naturally to her that she jokes, "Instead of brains, I may have circuitry and microchips inside my head. If I'd been born ten years earlier, I could have invented Facebook."

Would You Tell Us a Story About Yourself?

Telling stories is a most ordinary thing to do. After school you tell what happened that day. You tell friends what Donna said to Fred and how Kathy felt afterward.

The story you write for a college application isn't expected to be like a superbly crafted tale by Poe or O'Henry, just an autobiographical account of an experience. It should tell about something that happened and what it meant to you. A good story both entertains and informs the reader. A story written on a college application does even more. It suggests your values, clarifies your attitudes, and, better yet, brings you to life in the admissions office.

Although storytelling possibilities are limitless, application questions usually direct you to identify and discuss a noteworthy time in your life:

—Write an original essay about a humorous personal experience.

—What is it that you have done that best reflects your personality?

—Describe a challenging situation and how you responded.

—Comment on an experience that helped you discern or define a value you hold.

—What is the most difficult thing you've ever done?

—Write about a group endeavor in which you participated, and describe your contribution.

In response to any of these topics, you can write a story about last night or pick an event from the time you were a small child. The experience can have been instantaneous or long-lived, a once-in-a-lifetime occasion or a daily occurrence. It can have taken place in a schoolroom, a ballroom, a mountaintop— anywhere, in fact, including inside your head.

An event need not have been earthshaking to inspire a story. Almost everything you do from the moment you wake up holds possibilities. If you haven't noticed how life is crammed with moments of drama, cast off those blurry lenses and start to look for the hidden realities behind the daily face of things: In a dis- agreement with your brother, in an

> Almost anything you do from the moment you wake up has possibilities.

encounter with a former girlfriend or boyfriend, or in a teacher's criticism you may find the ingredients for an insightful, dramatic essay. Simply by making a list of ten things that happened yester- day and another ten things that occurred last week, you may trig- ger more than one essay idea.

DO . . .

   ✓ Answer the question that is asked.

   ✓ Choose an experience you remember well. Details will make or break your story.

✓ Pick an experience you can dramatize. Let the reader hear people speaking and see people acting!

✓ Focus on a specific incident or event.

✓ Make yourself the central character in the story.

DON'T . . .

✗ Think that a commonplace event can't be turned into an uncommonly good story.

✗ Choose a complicated event unless you can explain it briefly. Fill in background, but focus on what happened.

✗ Bore your readers with a rambling tale that goes nowhere.

✗ Explain your point with a lecture on what the reader is supposed to notice. Let the story make its own point.

Answers That Worked

Ted B collects things: antique license plates, matchbook covers, and rocks. From his hobby he has learned about design, geography, advertising, and geology—and interior decorating, too, for after five years of collecting, he literally wallpapered the foyer of his house with matchbook covers.

Megan M faced a serious dilemma when Stacey, a Facebook friend from another state, grew increasingly depressed and hinted that she's considered taking her own life. Alarmed and scared, Megan didn't know what to do. Should she try to comfort Stacey by herself? Or would it be better to alert her parents and thereby betray her friend's trust? After realizing how awful it would be to lose a friend she might have saved, Megan contacted Stacey's mother. To this day, Megan remains torn about her decision.

Pete S was riding in a car with his brother. At a stoplight a pretty girl in a neighboring car smiled at him. Pete looked away. Afterward, he berated himself and resolved to become more outgoing and more assertive—with mixed results.

Colin V is Catholic. Last year on May 6th his Jewish godson was born. As a result, Colin's eyes have been opened to the world of Jewish customs. "I look at my religion differently now," Colin wrote.

Jenny B's hard-of-hearing grandfather lives with the family. Whenever Jenny tries to help the old man, he rebuffs her. A blowup occurred after Jenny knocked too loudly on his door to summon him to the phone. The incident has caused her to reflect at length on the needs of her grandfather and other aging people.

Mary G, from a middle-income family, works in a slum area soup kitchen with her church group. She'll never be a social reformer, but the work, she claims, has made her "more sensitive to the lives of the poor and homeless."

Roy O's summer in the country with his father preparing a hillside for a future vineyard gave him time to think about how lucky he was to have been born in the United States into a fairly well-to-do family. "I'll never take the blessings of life for granted again," he wrote.

Liz H and her twin sister Mary have rarely been apart. Lately, Liz has found it necessary to seek her own identity and has taken up running as a way to get away. Her hours of solitude on the road have helped to strengthen the bonds with her sister.

Lucy C says, "Sunday is always spent gathering the scattered fragments of my life." It's the day she uses to catch up on schoolwork, gain some perspective on her social life, make peace with her parents, and look in the mirror for a long time trying to figure out who she is.

Lauren S has always been plagued by insecurity. An offhand remark by an art teacher ("Hey, you're good!") has helped her to build confidence and work that much harder in her courses. She's beginning to see signs of how good she really is.

Maria R's parents were divorced. The complex legal negotiations that accompanied the split, while painful to her, so fascinated Lisa that she plans to become a lawyer.

Max S thinks that he has been ostracized at his school because of his ragged appearance. Instead of wearing a jacket and tie to an honor society interview, he showed up in a black leather jacket and torn jeans. The incident heightened his awareness that people are judged by superficialities, not by their character.

What Is Important to You?

Would you rather listen to a Bach cantata or a Guns 'n Roses album? Would you prefer to blog or spend an afternoon in an art museum? Do you like fast foods or nouvelle cuisine? To a great extent, your preferences define you. Hoping for a glimpse of your taste and your biases, many colleges ask you to write a "choice" essay. Rather than give you a menu of choices, however, they tell you to come up with one of your own—your favorite quotation or word, an historical event you would like to have changed, a significant book you've read:

—What is your favorite quotation? Explain your choice.
—What have you read that has had special significance for you? Explain.
—What is your favorite noun? What does it mean to you?
—If you could invent anything, what would you create? Discuss.

—If you could affect the outcome of human history by changing a particular event, what event would you choose? How would you change it, and why?

—If you could spend an evening with any prominent person—living, deceased, or fictional—whom would you choose, and why?

What you choose when responding to such questions is important. But the rationale for your choice is even more important and should make up the heart of your essay.

The key to writing a forceful response is that your choice has some direct, personal bearing on your life. A quotation from Shakespeare may sound impressive, but if you pick it only for effect, you'd be better off with a lyric from Shania Twain or a maxim of your grandmother's. If you write on a book, don't limit yourself to school reading. What you've read on your own tells far more about you than any class assignment.

If your first response to a question is, "Oh, that's an easy one!" ask yourself if the same "easy" answer might not be popping into a thousand other minds across the country. Then set your sights on a less obvious answer. Conversations with Columbus, Benjamin Franklin, John Lennon, and Barack Obama have already been written. So have numerous essays about inventing cures for cancer and AIDS. Many students have already written about altering human history by eliminating war, preventing the birth of Hitler, and stopping the 9/11 hijackers. Frankly, admissions staffers sigh wearily over essays on overused topics.

The good news, however, is that it's not impossible to write a sparkling essay on an ordinary subject. A fresh, honest, and thoughtfully-written essay, regardless of its subject, is always welcome in college admissions offices.

DO . . .

✓ Answer the question that is asked.

✓ Choose a subject that you care about.

✓ Let your head and heart be your source of material.

✓ Think of at least three very good personal reasons for your choice.

✓ Try out more than one answer. Submit the one that you like best.

DON'T . . .

✗ Choose a topic merely to look good.

✗ Be self-conscious about your choice. Just tell the truth.

✗ Choose a subject that requires research. Let your experience guide you.

Answers
That
Worked

Sabrina S is the drum major of her school's marching band. She recalls a time when she thought that winning competitions was the band's only purpose. As a senior, she realizes that there's more to it than collecting trophies. The band has become an essential part of her life. "The school parking lot became my 'home' and the members of the band have become my 'family,'" she wrote.

Barbara B has been fascinated with space flight ever since second grade when the elementary school librarian introduced her to a science fiction book, *Matthew Looney, the Boy from the Moon*. In college Barbara expects to major in physics and then join a company that builds space vehicles.

Luke J chose the word *family* as his favorite noun. To explain, he wrote a moving portrait of a close-knit family. Five times in the last ten years the family has moved. Luke's father works overseas for months at a time. Yet, Luke derives stability from his family, despite its fragmented lifestyle.

Mitch B refuted the old adage, "You can't compare apples and oranges," by writing a tongue-in-cheek comparison of the two fruits. As a result, he wonders about the validity of other pieces of wisdom. He plans to research next "You can't tell a book by its cover" and "Absence makes the heart grow fonder."

Carl G, who has a deaf younger brother, wrote about *Dancing without Music—Deafness in America,* a book that persuaded him and his parents to introduce young Danny to other deaf people as a way to help the boy find an identity as a hearing-impaired person.

Gary K wrote about Steven, his mentally retarded brother. All his life, Gary has been Steven's fun committee, psychiatrist-at-home, and teacher. Gary wept recently after he found Steven eating pineapple from a can. It had taken Gary six weeks to teach Steven how to use a can opener.

Joanna L wrote that there's nothing better than hearing the expression "Time's up" in gym class. As she put it, "Gym has always been intimidating to me. It has convinced me that physically I am, and always will be, a clumsy oaf. . . . The smell of a gymnasium and the sight of orange mats stimulate feelings of terror and dread."

Ian R said he'd like to have dinner with Bill Gates. "I identify with him," Ian wrote. "On the outside, he looks like a schnook, the guy next door who gets bullied on the school bus. I've always been (and I'm proud to admit it) somewhat nerdy myself." Ian goes on to explain that he'd ask Bill Gates to divulge the secret of how a nerd can become one of the richest and most powerful men in America.

Marley E picked Alfred Lansing's *Endurance: Shackleton's Incredible Voyage* as a book that had special significance for him. Shackleton, an Antarctic explorer, survived with his crew for five months on a drifting ice pack in one of the most treacherous areas in the world. "The determination of the men to survive is awe-inspriring," wrote Marley. "They endured incredible suffering with superhuman courage. Their inspirational story made me aware as never before of the potential of humans to overcome physical and emotional hardship. As a result of reading this book, my opinion of humanity has taken a giant leap forward and strengthened my own resolve to succeed in life."

What Would You Like to Tell Us About Yourself?

Perhaps the toughest question is the one without a suggested topic:

—We would welcome any comments you care to make about yourself.

—The essay is an important part of your application. It will help admissions officers gain a more complete picture of you. Use the essay to tell about yourself.

—If there is anything else you would like to tell us about you, please explain on an additional sheet.

—Please use this page to give us any information you think would be helpful to us as we consider your application.

—The purpose of this application is to help us learn about you.

—Is there additional information we should know that will help us to make an informed decision?

—To better understand you, what else should we know?

Without restrictions, you may literally send in anything. Starting from scratch, you can cook up a totally new piece of writing. Or you may submit a poem, a story, or a paper you've written for school or yourself. Applicants who have written for publications often send samples of their writing. If you include a previously written piece, don't just pull it from your files and throw it in the envelope. Carefully explain on a new cover page what it is and why you chose it.

In response to this question, one applicant to Ohio Wesleyan sent in a scrapbook of his experience as a congressional committee witness on children's health care, a matter that affected him personally. To the admissions committee, this was a compelling statement about his dedication and ability to advocate for something he believed, even at a relatively young age.

Although colleges say they want to know you better, you don't have to reveal an intimate secret about yourself. Applicants have sent in essays about child abuse, divorce, anorexia, surviving cancer—you name it. Essay readers are moved by human tragedy no more and no less than the rest of us, but they won't lower their admission standards because you have suffered. Rather, they look for applicants who can reflect on their hardships with wisdom and maturity. They're aware of human misery, but they look for more than the fact that you went through a bad experience. They want to know what you think about it now.

DO . . .

✓ Pick something important—something that matters to you.

✓ Consider explaining anything unusual that has influenced your school or home life.

✓ Use a style of writing that sounds like you.

✓ Write the sort of piece (for example, essay, poem, internal monologue) that you've written successfully in the past.

DON'T . . .

✗ Turn down the college's invitation to write more about yourself.

✗ Put on airs to try to impress the college. Be yourself.

✗ Repeat what you've written elsewhere on your application.

✗ Try to use a form or style of writing for the first time unless you have a record of successful writing experiments.

✗ Write the essay (or any other part of your application) the night before it's due.

Answers That Worked

Bonnie W asserted that writing the college essay helped her sort out her feelings about herself. She has finally accepted the fact that she is a nonconformist. "I used to run with the 'in' crowd," she wrote, "but now I don't give a damn. I can breathe."

Lillian S, a student of karate, wrote about how it feels to break a board with her bare hand. Writing about karate, she said, has heightened her concentration as she trains to earn a black belt.

———————

Dave E reflected on violence in America. His thoughts had been triggered by a triple murder that had occurred a few weeks earlier in a neighboring town.

———————

Kevin B wrote a funny piece on being a motorcycle enthusiast. On a recent trip to Massachusetts with the school band, his overnight host expected him to come equipped with a switchblade and chains. The folks in the Bay State seemed disappointed by his "normal" behavior and appearance.

———————

Jenny J wrote a collection of fables, each concluding with a moral or maxim to illustrate a strongly held conviction. One story ended, "Be satisfied with who you are." Another, "Don't turn your back on anyone in pursuit of power."

———————

Adam B wrote a piece detailing the first time he baked walnut tarts. Like an expectant father, he paced the kitchen floor, waiting for the oven bell to sound. At the gong, his whole family rushed in for a taste. The verdict? "Well, that night I retired with a grin on my face," wrote Adam.

———————

Ray G, a high school baseball player, wrote a tongue-in-cheek analysis of his statistics. Last season he batted .300. He also got 600 on his math SAT. "Does that mean my math is twice as good as my hitting?" Ray asked. "I doubt that my math teacher would say so," he added.

———————

Jodi F wrote about a family trip to Europe. Her parents were on the verge of separation, but during the tour of Italy, France, and Spain her mother and father made peace. "How odd," thought Jodi, "to save my home by leaving it."

Barry G wrote of waking in the middle of a hot summer night and going to the roof of his apartment building for some air. Peering at the lights below, he experienced a self-revelation. As an intelligent person, he realized that if he set his mind to it, he could do almost anything he wanted to with his life. Thinking of possibilities, he stayed on the roof until dawn.

Pamela M reviewed her dancing career since age four and concluded by stating, "Dancing has allowed me to express myself from within and to be, feel, and love who I am."

Martin S wrote about playing the piano. To show that he is a stellar pianist was not his point, however. Rather, he focused on the psychological differences he felt between playing for himself and playing for a public performance or a competition. "On my own," he wrote, "I don't have to control my mind so much. I can let intuitive hunches flow into my hands. A small inner voice speaks to me, allowing me to experience moments of real feeling or insight. Suddenly, highly-charged music far transcends the notes printed on the page."

Thinking of Ideas to Write About

If you're one of those blessed writers who explode with ideas for every assignment, read no further. You don't need this section. If, however, you routinely come back empty handed from topic searches, try some of these popular do-it-yourself techniques for spawning ideas:

1. If your essay due date is weeks or months away, start a journal today. Innumerable college essays have begun life as journal entries. From now on, record whatever catches your eye or tickles your brain. Anything! Since no one else will see what you write, literally everything is OK. Some of what you write may be silly and pointless, but not if you force yourself to tell the truth and only the truth.

   Frankly, your honest images and thoughts may lead to a dead end, but journal keepers often run into rich veins of ideas in their daily entries. After a few days, a journal begins to be a source book of information on you. When you need a topic for your college essay, you'll have a personal reference book at your fingertips. In its pages you may discover the stuff to write the essay of your life.

2. Try free-writing. That is, write nonstop for ten to fifteen minutes a day, paying no heed to grammar, spelling, or punctuation. Concentrate on telling the truth about whatever is on your mind that day. You'll be amazed at how rapidly ideas flow when you write unself-consciously and without preplanning. After free-writing you won't have a polished essay, or even a first draft, but you might have bagged one or two surprisingly fertile ideas.

3. Focus your free-writing. Once you have done some free-writing, reread what you've written. Circle any idea or phrase you like or that holds promise for an essay topic. Take one of the ideas that feels right, and free-write on that one. When you focus your free-writing, you accumulate possibilities on a topic. The human mind spits out thoughts so speedily that most of them vanish before they reach consciousness. In free-writing, though, you can preserve thoughts before they get away. Try focused free-writing again and again, until you've arrived at a satisfactory essay topic.

4. Like pulling out a stopper, making a list often starts the flow of ideas. A list of items, quickly jotted down, may bring to mind just the topic you're looking for. Writing down lists of influential people in your life or books you've read acts like a simple word-association exercise. As your mind makes connections, one name calls up memories of the next and the next. Anything and anyone can go on your list. At first, don't be particular. Later you can start to be discriminating as you narrow the choices for a possible essay topic.

5. On a very long sheet of paper—perhaps a roll of printer or art kraft paper—create a timeline of your life. Write down every event you can think of, whether you think it's important or not. Ask people whom you've known for a long time to suggest additional items for your time line. A perusal of the finished work may suggest lifelong themes, key events, and personal interests that can be turned into essay topics.

6. Talk to anyone who'll listen—a teacher or coach, a boss or a soulmate also in search of a topic. When you least expect it, one of you might just blurt out the very idea you've been looking for. Besides, when you solve a problem with someone else, you often get a bonus called synergism—the combined power of two heads working together, which usually exceeds the total power of two heads working separately.

3 AN ESSAY THAT WORKS

In a survey about "life's ten most anxious moments," a majority of high school seniors agreed that getting up to talk in front of a group provoked the most anxiety. Second was applying to college, especially writing the essay.

It's easy to see why. The two tasks—addressing a group and composing an essay for a college application—have a lot in common. In both cases success depends on how well you present yourself, what you have to say, and how effectively you convey your message. Few people don't feel at least a little stage fright before facing an audience, and it's equally natural to feel edgy about filling up an empty computer screen with an essay that could clear or block your entry to your college of choice.

But, if you can be objective about it, you don't need to get into a sweat over your essay. Once you have a handle on what colleges expect, once you know the pitfalls to avoid and are psyched to do a good job, the application essay won't be all that intimidating. Yes, it will take time and energy—but with any luck, the payoff will be well worth it.

Essay Tips

As you go about preparing, writing, and editing your essay, keep in mind the following basic tips. Although some of them are pretty obvious, they have helped countless college applicants conquer their essay-writing anxiety.

- **Start early**. Give yourself a long head start. The summer between junior and senior year is perfect. Free from the pressures of school and other obligations, use your days in the sun to think about a topic. Test out your essay ideas informally with chat groups and other people whose judgment you trust. Use the time to read books like this one and to study successful sample essays found in print or online. (*The sample essays and essay excerpts in this book should help—a lot.*)
- **Cast aside preconceptions of what a college wants**. Don't assume that admissions officials want anything but an honest piece of writing. (*See page 62 for more on the perils of trying too hard to guess essay readers' expectations.*)

- **Answer the question**. You'd be surprised at how many applicants miss the point of the question and dash off marginally-related essays.

- **Avoid clichés**. That is, don't write the same essay that could also be written by other applicants. Rather, devise something new and fresh and engaging, something that will help you stand out in a crowd of hundreds, or even thousands, of other applicants. (*See pages 66–68 for tips on writing a unique essay.*)

- **Choose a tone that speaks well of you**. Colleges favor thoughtful applicants with optimistic, confident, agreeable personalities. Avoid boasting, whining, groveling, sarcasm, and self-pity. (*See pages 69–71 for tips on the boasting problem.*)

- **Write a well-organized, detailed essay that focuses on a single main idea**. By limiting your topic, you improve the odds of hooking your readers' interest. (*See pages 92–94 and 100–113 on composing a readable essay.*)

- **Follow the conventions of standard English usage and grammar**. Use your computer's spell-checker and proofread your essay again and again. (*Turn to pages 145–146 on presenting a competently-written essay.*)

- **Think about your audience**. Put yourself in the shoes of your readers and ask whether anything you wrote might be unclear or ambiguous. (*See pages 114–146 for guidelines on editing your essay.*)

- **Stick to the word limit**. If a college says write between 250 and 500 words, give them them what they asked for—no fewer and no more. (*See pages 145–146 for more on following directions.*)

- **Get feedback from others**. Let others—teachers, counselors, friends, family—read your essay and tell you in detail what your words convey about you. (*See pages 146–148 for a discussion of getting outside help.*)

Write Honestly

Nicole T, a high school senior interested in Saint Lawrence University, dealt with her stress by trying to guess what the admissions office would expect her to write in response to Topic #1, the "identity" question on the Common App." She searched Saint Lawrence's Web pages for clues to what the college might like and found in its statement of core values the phrase "environmental sustainability." Reading further, Nicole discovered that the university hoped to foster "innovative alternatives to car-based commuting."

> Success depends on how well you present yourself, what you have to say and how effectively you convey your message.

"They probably mean the use of bicycles as a way to reduce greenhouse gases," Nicole decided. "Well, if they're that green, I'll give them a very bright-green applicant." So, she set out to write an essay to prove that, because of their mutual interest in saving the planet, she and Saint Lawrence were meant for each other. Her opening paragraph read:

> Your website said that you are supporting environmental sustainability by promoting modes of transportation to reduce the use of cars. I would like to attend Saint Lawrence because that description fits me perfectly. I have been an avid bike rider for years. I am the type of person who goes everywhere on my bike—to school, to dance classes, to visit friends and family. I am happier while biking than doing almost anything else. Last summer I did a 400-mile ride to raise money for AIDS.

In the rest of her essay, Nicole highlighted various events that took place during her AIDS bike ride.

Nicole had the academic credentials for Saint Lawrence, but was rejected. She had made the fatal mistake of trying to guess what she thought the college wanted, an approach always filled with peril. Admissions people don't want anything in particular except to have applicants write something that accurately portrays themselves. Applicants "shouldn't try to figure out what a school is looking for," says Harvard's admissions director Marlyn McGrath Lewis. "They should just try to convey a real and memorable sense of themselves." Lewis's words are echoed in essay instructions from

> Nicole made the mistake of trying to guess what the college wanted.

M.I.T., which say, "Remember that this is not a writing test. . . . Be honest, be open, be authentic—this is your opportunity to connect with us. You should certainly be thoughtful about your essays, but if you're thinking too much—spending a lot of time stressing or strategizing about what makes you 'look best,' as opposed to the answers that are honest and easy—*you're doing it wrong.*"

Thus, when an application question asks, "Who belongs on a modern-day Mount Rushmore?"—as the College of William and Mary once did—there really is no "correct" answer.

In an essay concerning a significant accomplishment, Susan E gave Yale an honest self-portrait. Writing about her audition for a summer school in the arts, she said,

> The tryouts were not unlike writing a college essay. Acting is, after all, the art of revealing character, and that is what I am trying to do now: present a clear picture of Susan E's character . . . so, if you don't mind, I'm going to think of this whole affair as an audition.
>
> Actually, my experience with acting auditions is very limited. The most memorable and important audition I have ever had was for a summer theater program that I attended after my junior year. There were two auditions, a semifinal and a final round, and each time I performed two dramatic monologues. I created other people's characters and spoke other people's words. Thinking back on the experience, I believe my own character and my own words would have been infinitely more interesting. . . .

Susan then quoted the monologue and described her feelings after the audition:

> There's the tremendous feeling of accomplishment. I suppose that's a big part of it—the accomplishment. I don't imagine performing would stimulate me so much if I had no success at it. In fact, if I were lousy at it, I probably would stay clear of it as much as possible—like gym. . . . Yeah, failure generally stinks. It's very scary to fail. In fact, right about now I'm going to start the seemingly unending process of contemplating this audition. "Did it go well? Did I say too much? Was I too honest? Did I sound silly? Will they laugh about this for weeks to come?"—Paranoia strikes deep, but fear of failure strikes deeper. Then I'll go the other way: "Of course they liked you. Honesty is refreshing. It took guts to be silly and they'll respect you for it." Well, I guess I'll know soon enough.

There's more, but by now you've probably noticed that there's an honest-to-goodness person writing the words here. Susan's essay could be an entry in her diary—it's that personal. It's the kind of writing that helps application readers set one applicant apart from the others. In fact, that's the whole point, says Carol A. Rowlands, associate dean of admissions at Lafayette. "An essay should distinguish one applicant from another."

Write About Something Important to You

By creating a false persona in your essay, you're being dishonest, posing as someone you are not. An imposter may try to pass himself off in his essay as a seriously committed poet. But if the rest of his application makes no reference to writing poetry, or working on publications, or taking poetry courses, readers may think twice about accepting his word. Consistency helps. Admissions officials often cite cases of students who write impassioned essays about racism, sweatshop labor, the plight of the homeless, gun laws, and other timely issues. Yet nothing in the students' records shows a particular interest in human rights, in politics, or in any current issues for that matter. Topics seem to have been pulled from the pages of newspapers.

Application essays are not meant to demonstrate your knowledge of current events. They have an altogether different purpose. "Pick a topic you care about, an issue of significance and familiarity to you," says John E. Stafford, a professional guidance counselor in New York. Why? Because nothing will flop faster than an impersonal essay full of sweeping generalizations about a big issue that has puzzled experts and politicians for years. If you're going to write about the homeless, make sure you can demonstrate real knowledge and personal interest. Have you, for example, served dinner in a downtown shelter, collected clothing for homeless families, or at least spoken out about the subject in your history class? Monica Barbano, a former admissions official at Muhlenberg, advises, "Write about something you feel strongly about, something you're

> Before you write about the homeless, serve dinner in a downtown shelter.

passionate about—and not only will you be excited about it, so will we."

Andy C, applying to the University of Vermont, botched a one-and-a-half page essay on issues of global warming that began this way:

> · In this day and age environmental problems are very important worldwide topics of discussion. These controversial issues have a great effect on all of society. In particular, the depletion of the ozone layer is affecting the future of mankind's habitat. In the last fifty years, the polar ice caps have receded in record amounts. . . .

Andy was probably sincere, perhaps even gravely worried about global warming, but the start of his essay shows nothing personal or passionate about his concern.

Harry Bauld, a former admissions dean at Brown and Columbia, says that vague statements that go on and on about pollution, AIDS, or world hunger are called "Miss America" essays. Like beauty queens, they recite platitudes and offer simple-minded solutions to the stickiest problems. "I think the conflict between pro-life and pro-choice could be solved if both sides just sat down and had a good heart-to-heart talk," wrote one "contestant" in an application sent to Boston University.

In contrast, Inga K, applying to Johns Hopkins, laid claim to a serious interest in Finnish politics at the outset of an essay on the Finnish economy:

> Through my mother I am a Finnish citizen. A native of Finland, she wanted her children to hold dual citizenship. . . .
> Even though I am very Americanized, I still have strong ties to Finland. At home I often speak Finnish, I eat Finnish food, read Finnish magazines, and even subscribe to a Helsinki newspaper online. Although I have a lot of American friends, I'm closer to the Finnish friends I have at my church. Each summer I go to Finland for about a month to visit my relatives. When I am older, I may go to there to live. I don't know yet.
> Lately, I have been watching closely the Finnish economy and the consequences of growing unemployment . . .

"The best essays," says Susan Wertheimer, associate director of admissions at the University of Vermont, "come directly from the heart. Too often, students think we want to read only about 'big' themes or major life events. That's not so. One of the most memorable essays I've read was composed by a young woman who described her feelings when her best friend moved away. The topic was simple—a common experience in today's mobile culture. I understood how she felt, why the friendship had meant so much to her, how she'd coped with the loss and moved on in her life."

Write a Unique Essay—the One That Only You Can Write

Essays on topics of consuming personal interest don't always guarantee success. Sometimes you can hardly tell one from the other. They sound almost mass-produced. "We don't expect Pulitzer Prize essays," says Karen Ley, a former admissions associate at Lafayette, "just good honest efforts that tell us something about the individual writer."

When he began his essay for the Air Force Academy, Tom M didn't realize the pitfalls of assembly-line writing:

> I would like to attend the Air Force Academy because I want a good college education. I also want to learn to fly, become a military officer and serve my country.

"So do 8,000 other applicants," Tom's high school English teacher told him. "What's going to set you apart from every other candidate?" It was fortunate that Tom ran his essay through several drafts. His first effort would certainly have earned him a letter of rejection because it lacked a hook to catch the attention of an admissions official. Much later, after numerous drafts, Tom had a hook:

> "Five. Four. Three. Two. One. Blast off!"
> My friend Eric pushed the button and a red rocket, about as long as my forearm and less than half as wide, whooshed into the sky. It almost disappeared from view before we saw the opening of a small white parachute that would bring it safely back to earth. "Wow-eee," Eric and I shouted as we sprinted toward the landing site as fast as our eleven-year-old legs would move. Another successful launch by the founders and only members of the Linden Street Junior Birdman Club!

Tom then recalls that his love affair with flying sprouted during his days as a rocket freak in sixth grade. Although Tom finally decided not to apply to the Air Force Academy, the magnetism of his new opening paragraph would probably have stopped his file from slipping unnoticed into the pile marked "Reject."

Jim R, an applicant to Duke, responding to the question, "What is it you do that best reflects your personality?" devised a uniquely personal approach. He wrote a list of forty sentences, each beginning with *I*:

> I love music of every kind.
> I have never been rock-climbing, but I intend to go soon.
> I share a room with my kid brother who is a dirt-bike maniac and who often drives me up the wall.
> I hate to sit in front of people who talk in the movies.
> I grow weepy over stories of faithful dogs like Lassie and Buck.
> I could survive very well on a diet of spaghetti and Dr Pepper.

Thirty-four sentences later, no reader could fail to recognize Jim, the person behind the essay.

When a college asks you to describe your interests, be cautious. Don't let your passion for karate, military history, or sailing distract you from the purpose of the essay—to show yourself to the college. Stay clear of the temptation to write a *Wikipedia* article on black belts, famous battles, or boats. Matt S couldn't resist writing about the subject he loved the most. He began (and continued) in this fashion:

> One of my main interests is cartography. Some day I hope to work for the U.S. Coast and Geodetic Survey, the federal agency responsible for making and maintaining maps for the government and the public. Mapmaking is fascinating, especially because maps keep changing. Most people think that the land never changes, but with road construction, dams, floods, earthquakes, storms and fires, many maps made forty or fifty years ago are now obsolete. One of the most dramatic cartographic changes in the United States has been on Cape Cod, Massachusetts. Every decade the ocean coastline recedes thirty feet and the bay shoreline grows a similar amount. The place where the pilgrims landed in 1620 is now a quarter of a mile offshore.

Few high school students study maps as avidly as Matt. In spite of his unusual passion, however, his essay sounds much like a geography textbook. Although a college seeking geography majors might love this, it fails to convey the qualities that admissions officials look for in application essays: ability to think on an abstract level, resilience, empathy, and a host of other *personal* qualities. Unfortunately, Matt hid his personality behind facts and statistics that say nothing about his upbeat, fun- and life-loving disposition.

Focus on a Single Area

Here is the opening paragraph of Nancy B's essay for Ohio Wesleyan:

> My four years in high school have been very rewarding and productive. I have become involved in many of the extracurricular activities offered at the school. In addition to academic achievements, I have developed a strong sense of leadership, evident in the positions I have held during the past four years as elected representative to the school government, captain of the lacrosse team, co-chair of the assemblies committee and editor-in-chief of the yearbook. . . .

Don't repeat in your essay what you've written someplace else on your application.

Because Nancy listed her school activities elsewhere on the application, she squandered a chance to give her readers additional information about herself. She masked a lively personality behind a façade of lifeless facts. Shirley Levin, an educational consultant from Rockville, Maryland, says, "An application essay should convey a feeling of pride, achievement, or accomplishment in a very small area."

Elissa G did just that in her Bryn Mawr application. Long a frustrated math student, she focused sharply on her ultimate victory over arithmetic, as this excerpt shows:

> . . . I never did get the hang of adding anything with more than one digit. I still have to think twice when multiplying six and eight. Moreover, I am completely reliant on my pencil and paper. The most annoying facet of this whole disability is that I understand and like math. Algebraic theory fascinated me, geometric proofs thrilled me and logarithms were amazing.

Yet, I kept messing up tests and problems because I multiplied wrong, or added wrong or subtracted wrong . . . thank heaven for partial credit! Finally, in my sophomore year, I was rewarded for my rudimentary deficiencies. After maintaining a B average in my Trig class for a whole year, I whizzed the Regents, got a 100 and received an A in the course.

Focusing on a single area may be tough when you've done a lot with your life. By targeting one activity, though, you can show how hard you've thrown yourself into it. You can also include specific details about yourself, details that make you sound more like a real person. Consider, for example, this excerpt from Susan F's essay for Brown University:

My most rewarding acting experience was at the Andover Summer Session. I played the ruinous young girl, Mary Tilford, in Lillian Hellman's *The Children's Hour*. The role was very different from those I was accustomed to, like the good-natured nurse, Nellie Forbush, in *South Pacific*. Mary is a sadistic, tantrum-throwing, spoiled child who can also present a most ingenuous exterior. To show her complex personality—the manipulative female, the affectionate grandchild, the nasty friend—was difficult for me. I have a tendency to repress all anger, and when Mary was alone with her peers she was vicious. In one scene I had to slap a girl who is a good friend. To make the slap believable I had to really hit her. This was almost harder than the hysterics or the cloying sweetness, but with practice was finally perfected. To my pleasure, some of the audience did take my portrayal seriously. I had several students stop me in the cafeteria and with horrified expressions exclaim, "You're so mean!" Fiction had been transformed into reality—perhaps the best review.

The Boasting Problem

Susan wanted Brown to know of her triumph on the stage. She was rightfully proud of her accomplishment, yet didn't sound boastful. Most of us try not to puff ourselves up too much. We don't want to appear conceited. Still, Shirley Levin reminds college applicants, "Look, if

> Be proud of your achievements, but don't brag.

you don't blow your horn, nobody else will." The problem, though, is that self-impressed people rarely impress others. So, if you're good at something, tell the college, of course, but don't shout. A champion with a touch of reserve or a sense of humor is always more endearing than a big-mouthed braggart.

Mike M is a gifted political cartoonist, justifiably proud of his accomplishments. He injects droll humor into all his drawings. Yet in this passage from his New York University essay, which focuses on his gift, he sounds smug, even arrogant:

> I would like to direct the attention of the admissions committee to my extensive involvement in political cartooning for the past four years. The responsibility of producing no less than one satirical drawing per week has necessitated my regular reading of *The New York Times* and other news publications, such as *Time* and *USA Today*. As a consequence, I have become well-informed on issues of national affairs and American foreign policy. In the future, I anticipate using my knowledge and artistic talent to raise the social consciousness of the ordinary citizen by pointing out the issues that I feel are of great importance.

Mike was accepted, but surely not for being the sort of person his essay portrays.

Similarly, a high school senior named Eliot M, evidently dazzled by his own musical achievement, didn't realize how immodest he sounded when he told Tufts:

> My extraordinary talent and accomplishments in the field of music are sufficiently noteworthy to warrant my inclusion in the highly selective all-county orchestra.

Although Eliot may deserve respect for his musicianship, he could probably use a lesson in modesty.

Actually, modesty is rather easy to learn. Just say that you consider yourself lucky to have great talent, or after telling how you've struggled to attain success, add that you're still trying to do better. For instance, Suzanne W, another exceptional musician, wrote on her Yale application:

> As a violinist, I have discovered wonderful feelings of accomplishment, surpassed only by the knowledge that it is only the beginning of a lifetime's experience.

Roger D is also blessed with excellence. He loves art and knows a lot about it. In his Columbia essay, he showed how well informed he is by relating an incident in the art museum:

> As I was standing in front of *St. Francis in Ecstasy*, two college students came over and started discussing the painting because they had to answer questions about its symbolism, composition and use of color for their art history class. Realizing that they weren't getting very far on their own, I decided to help. I pointed out religious symbolism and mentioned Giovanni Bellini's influence on Venetian painting—his use of sensuous colors and perspective. They · seemed impressed by what I said, and I don't know which I enjoyed more—talking about the painting or looking at it.

The simple phrase, "I don't know," rescues Roger from sounding vain. What gave his spirits even more of a boost was that he used his knowledge to do a good turn for someone else.

Of course, excessive pride may not be your problem. Like most people, perhaps, you don't have an exceptional talent. In fact, you may be searching for something in your life that's worth writing about. Don't worry. Everyday life has been the source of many outstanding essays. In your school locker, in your work as a cashier at Target, in your close ties to a grandparent, you may find kindling for a good, sharply focused essay. For Tufts, Dave K wrote about delivering newspapers to lonely senior citizens. Every day he became an old woman's link to the world. Kenny D, applying to Michigan, described his fight against boredom as a stock clerk at a supermarket. As he unpacked boxes he became a student of shopping carts, discovering that consumers express themselves by their choice of groceries.

Dangerous Areas: Proceed with Caution

Although no subject is totally off-limits, some essay topics contain pitfalls that you should avoid. The reason is that admissions people look for distinctive essays—that is, essays that somehow stand apart from the rest. Yet, countless cliché-ridden essays about common summer-camp experiences, extracurricular activities, a favorite grandparent, scoring the winning goal, a trip to Mexico, and many other popular subjects continue to be submitted by applicants who failed to understand the fact that, even if they choose a conventional topic, they must try to give it a fresh slant, one that illustrates their maturity and ability to think uniquely.

The "Jock" Essay

Admissions personnel are rarely impressed by the so-called jock essay, the one that predictably tells the reader what you learned from being first-string left tackle or playing goalie on the field hockey team. Every reasonably successful athlete has learned self-discipline, courage, and sportsmanship on the field. If a sport has truly been a crucial part of your life, your essay will have to show how. But you'll have to do more than write the story of how winning the race made you feel, or how losing it helped to build your character.

In her application essay for the University of North Carolina, Alison L, a sprinter on the track team who suffers from exercise-induced asthma, wrote that "the word 'fun' had no place in the lexicon of track terms, while the phrase 'welcome to Hell' found itself right at home." Her essay details the agony of daily practice but then bursts with gratitude for all the benefits she derived from pushing herself to the limit:

> It is said that the strength of effort is the measure of the result, and by golly, I must have made one heck of an effort because the long-term results are wonderful and abundant. The most significant effect is the impact track has made on my health. While running, I could not conceive how the strain I was placing on my already burdened lungs could possibly improve my condition, but I soon realized that intense training expanded my lung capacity, increased my endurance, improved my muscular strength, and on top of it all, caused me to lose thirteen excess pounds.

Alison adds that track improved her performance in school, too. Before track, she procrastinated and always rushed to complete homework at the last minute. "While on the team," she wrote, "I was forced to finish assignments many days prior to the due date, in anticipation of lengthy track meets."

Brian C, a fencer, wrote a more dramatic jock essay for the University of Pennsylvania. As these excerpts show, Brian invites you into his mind during a match:

"Fencers, ready?"

"Ready, sir."

"Fence!"

. . . I must win this bout. I have to be careful; I must find and exploit his weakness without allowing him to ensnare me with his strength. Every fencing bout starts like an argument: In the beginning, one must be patient and find out where one's opponent stands on the issue, before going in for the kill. When I was a child I would always lose arguments. Afterward I would go home and think of things I could have said to win. When I entered high school, I joined Model Congress, an organization patterned on the U.S. Congress. After three years, it has improved my verbal fencing immeasurably and I find that now I rarely lose an argument.

. . . He advances; I retreat, extend, lunge and miss. He moves in for the riposte. Panicking, I make a wild parry; he coolly disengages and I feel his point on my chest.

"Halt!" yells the director. "Touch left. Score is 3–1. Fencers ready?"

I am upset. He's scored three times as many touches on me as I have on him. If the bout continues like this, I will lose! This sport is silly; poking people with metal blades! I could be reading a book now. Reading is a wonderful pastime because every time I read I learn something new. When I read, I empathize with the characters. I feel new feelings and think new thoughts. Every book I read makes me more complete.

As he thrusts and parries, Brian also thinks about skiing, sailing, doing his physics homework, and traveling. In fewer than 500 words, Brian's personality and interests unfold. He reveals his intellect and sense of humor, his versatility, and writing skill. Because he wrote a multidimensional self-portrait, Brian has strengthened his application. After reading the essay, an admissions committee would have little difficulty deciding whether Brian belonged in their college.

Last Summer I Went to . . .

At almost any college, Brian's essay would outclass most others, especially those written on such common topics as athletics, working as a camp counselor, a wilderness adventure, and travel. Traveling, in fact, is among the most popular subjects

Travel is a popular subject for college application essays.

chosen for college essays. Applicants using the Common App seem extraordinarily fond of turning their travels into essays about places where they felt perfectly content (Topic #4) or an event that marked their transition from childhood to adulthood (Topic #5). Travel has virtues galore, but writing about it can be perilous. Colleges take a dim view of essays that turn out to be little more than personal narratives of "My Trip to Niagara Falls" or "What I Learned About Myself While Biking the Berkshires." The admissions offices at the University of Virginia and other colleges report that one out of every five essays seems to be about travel. Karen Ley, while working on the admissions staff at Lafayette, read thirty accounts of summer trips in a single day. "I never knew that travel could be so tedious," she recalls.

Once in a while, though, someone writes a gem of a travel essay, like the one Dylan M sent to Berkeley:

> I've lived my whole life on an ordinary street in an ordinary house that looks pretty much like every other house in town. So, when I got the chance to get away last summer, I set out to roam California on a bicycle with my friend Brett. Week after week we crisscrossed the state and camped out at night. We had hoped to find odd jobs to pay our food expenses but a depressed economy worked against us. Discouraged and almost broke after more than two weeks on the road, we were about to give up and go home when a man in a pick-up truck pulled up alongside us as we rested one afternoon in a park near Red Bluff.
>
> "You boys had lunch?" the driver asked.
>
> "Hardly had breakfast," I replied, so the man invited Brett and me to a nearby diner. Over hamburgers with cole slaw he made us an offer we couldn't refuse.
>
> "I'm doing some work on my property over near Payne's Creek, about 15 miles east of here," he said, "and I need some help. If you boys can give me a couple of days' work, I'll feed you and pay each of you a hundred dollars a day."
>
> "What kind of work?" I asked.
>
> "Construction. I'm building a small timber-frame house and need a hand lifting some of the posts and beams."
>
> "Done," said Brett without hesitating. Neither of us had the foggiest idea what the guy was talking about, but the prospect of hundreds of dollars in our pockets was irresistible.
>
> We shook hands all around. "Van's the name," he said.

Dylan goes on to describe the building process and how Van, evidently a master craftsman, showed the boys how to join large timbers to each other and to construct the frame of a house. The three days of sunup to sundown labor, Dylan writes, were "the hardest, sweatiest work I'd ever done." His essay closes with this paragraph:

> At night, we rolled out our sleeping bags on the floor of Van's house. At first, two wall frames stood above us, looking in the moonlight like the ruins of an ancient temple. The next night, we slept between four wall frames and a handful of rafters that we had helped Van lift into place. The timbers, while limiting our view of the Pleiades and the Big Dipper, outlined the shape of the house-to-be. On our last night, with a roof overhead, I felt like a different person than before. Helping to put a house together was an outrageous thing for me to be doing, but it gave me a surprising sense of accomplishment—even an emotional attachment to all those pieces of wood. Until then, I took houses for granted, my own included, never thinking about all the backbreaking effort and sweat that went into building them. I also never realized that an inanimate object like a house could generate such strong feelings in me. After each day in the sun I was tired, but it was a weariness different from the kind after an all-day bike ride or a day in school. It was way more satisfying because at the end I had something that could be seen and touched and would last a long time. It gave me a new perspective. Afterwards, I could hardly wait to return home, because I knew that to me, my ordinary house would never be ordinary again.

Dylan's travel piece differs from most others because it focuses on an encounter with just one person, Van. Notice, too, that the trip changed Dylan in a small way. It didn't alter his life or turn him into an adult overnight, but he now views his family home through more mature, experienced eyes. This is a modest change, far more credible than grandiose claims made by countless applicants that a summer trip forever reshaped their lives.

Unless you can make your travel story magical, store it in your scrapbook. Because some admissions counselors think that applicants who choose to tell about their travels are not pushing themselves creatively or intellectually, be sure you've found a fresh approach to your What-I-Did-Last-Summer essay. Don't turn an unforgettable summer adventure into a forgettable essay. For example, Tim C, an applicant to the University of Rochester, went traveling to New England and Canada, but his essay went nowhere, as this opening paragraph shows:

> An experience that has had a great meaning for me occurred the summer of my junior year. During that summer I spent a week in Maine, a week in Vermont, and a week in New Hampshire. I also visited Quebec for a briefer period of time. My trip away from home led me to mature and to obtain a better and broader picture of how other people live.

If Tim had left blank spaces where he wrote Maine, Vermont, and New Hampshire, you could fill in Maryland, Virginia, and North Carolina, or, for that matter, any other state or country on earth. The result would be the same—failure to convey the uniqueness of the experience.

Any essay that offers a stock response to a question is what Harry Bauld, a longtime reader of application essays, calls "the noose with which a seventeen-year-old can hang himself." In effect, such essays can work against you in the admissions office. Margaret Drugovich, past dean of admissions at Ohio Wesleyan University and now the president of Hartwick College, concurs. "Unique presentations are a welcome break from bundles of monotonous, repetitive essays," she observes, "and then almost always work to the student's advantage." To ensure that your essay will stand out, choose your topic with great care, particularly if you are inclined to write about travel or any other of the most popular topics, such as sports, family, friends, and the subject chosen by countless high school seniors—the pain and suffering that occur while writing an application essay.

> Don't turn an unforgettable summer adventure into a forgettable essay.

Answering the Offbeat Question

The University of Chicago's supplemental application asks a question invented by a team of undergraduates:

> "What does Play-Doh™ have to do with Plato?"
> Every May, the University of Chicago hosts the world's largest scavenger hunt. As part of this year's hunt, students

raced to find the shortest path between two seemingly unrelated things by traveling through Wikipedia articles. Wikipedia is so passé. Without the help of everyone's favorite collaborative Internet encyclopedia, show us your own unique path from Play-Doh™ to Plato.

Claremont McKenna College also enlists students to pose essay topics, for example:

> "Create a superhero who incorporates your best qualities: personality, talents, skills, etc. . . . what kind of superpowers would this superhero have . . . what is his or her name . . . what is his or her role in society . . . etc.?

Bennington College instructs you to "think out loud." That is, think aloud about something that's been on your mind for a while or something newly discovered. Then, use words, a sketch, a diagram—"any format that helps you express an idea." The admissions office at Emory University wants to know your favorite ride at the amusement park and how your choice reflects your approach to life.

Such questions aren't meant to stump or trick you. It doesn't matter to the folks at Bennington whether you develop your idea via a photo, a wood carving, or a cartoon. They just want to peek inside your head. When Colorado asks you to design a three-and-a-half-week intellectual adventure, they're obviously curious to know your interests and values. But they also want to know why you'd be driven to study migratory birds rather than, say, read plays by Tony Kushner or compare rights of defendants in American courts with the rights of defendants in other countries.

An offbeat question doesn't obligate you to write an offbeat answer. Essays that seem to have been written mainly to shock the reader or attract attention "are generally off-putting and tend to hide rather than showcase a candidate's special qualities," according to William M. Shain, past dean of admissions at Bowdoin, Vanderbilt, and Macalester. If you are naturally creative, write a creative essay, but if creativity is not your strong suit, write factually about your beliefs and feelings. You'll never be penalized for being honest and straightforward. "Above all," adds Shain, "avoid gimmicks. They almost never improve an essay." The high school quarterback who wrote his Columbia essay on a football did little to enhance his chances of being admitted. Nor did an Ohio Wesleyan applicant who for no apparent reason mailed in an essay attached to a coconut.

Beware of being too cute. If creativity isn't your strong suit, just be honest and straightforward.

If faced with an oddball question, beware of being too cute in your response. Some years ago, when Stanford asked, "What adjective do you think would be most frequently used to describe you by those who know you best?" one jokester replied, "terse," and didn't write the essay. University officials were not amused. In contrast, they were charmed by Elissa G's answer:

> It's a nice little word—"intriguing." It carries that suave nuance of smoky cafes and *Casablanca* or a James Bond movie. All of which are not exactly appropriate, since I could never imagine myself in a sleek, black evening gown, picking up a tall handsome guy in a wild, Latin nightclub only to have my romance completely spoiled by my father's kidnapping, etc. How boring. I'm not knocking the connotation though. I rather like being a dark and mysterious lady.
>
> Yet "intriguing" is just a bit more than a connotation. It's the ability to interest people and to keep them interested. It's a slightly contagious enthusiasm that interests people—that attracts them to you, your ideas, or your activities. That is something I certainly can do. For I can help triple the size of the Debate Team, or try something new with the yearbook, or surprise a close friend with an innovative idea . . . and with any luck, I can intrigue you.

In her first paragraph Elissa toys with the meaning of her word, but in the second she reveals its substance. Any admissions official would be "intrigued" by Elissa and want to know more about her.

Answering the Ordinary Question

An oddball essay question may inspire quirky answers but an ordinary question shouldn't tempt you to write an ordinary response. A typical question may ask, "What personal or academic experiences were particularly rewarding for you—a project, teacher, piece of writing or research, a particular course of study?" Although the question suggests that you write about

Take the less-traveled route; choose a topic that's distinctly yours.

school, you are free to pick any experience whatever. You may be better off, in fact, if you choose a unique personal experience. Finding your own topic demonstrates your initiative. You can also bet that most other people will play it safe and write about school. Don't run with the crowd—unless you know that you can beat them. Otherwise, take the less-traveled route. Choose a topic that is distinctly yours. (See Chapter 2 for lots of suggestions.)

Because unusual creativity is not essential, you can bring out your best in a sober, sensitive, and sincere essay as well. Just don't get caught in the trap of dry, long-winded and empty prose, like the writer who began his self-appraisal this way:

> During one's four years in secondary school, one's education
> is centered around a number of different things that hopefully
> will be helpful in college and in the career one pursues.

Yes, the point may be understandable, but the writing is dull and impersonal. Compare it to a more provocative statement like this:

> This whole college admission business is downright crazy.
> Very little of it has to do with education itself, and more with
> meeting deadlines, following procedures, and taking tests.
> So far, my image of college is a place dominated by rules
> and regulations and sorting students into categories accord-
> ing to some numeric scale. It makes me wonder if all that I
> learned in high school classes was a waste of time and
> effort. I sure hope not, but applying to college has prepared
> me to be disappointed.

At least you hear a person's voice in those words, and that's what colleges listen for.

College admissions people generally agree that the worst essays are those that summarize the writer's high school career. Nevertheless, students keep pumping out boring recitals of what they did since ninth grade. Such writers miss an opportunity to tell the college something distinctive about themselves. Their responses also suggest an inability to think deeply and to develop ideas about a single topic. Even worse, they reveal an unwilling-ness to take an intellectual risk, to extend themselves beyond the ordinary and mundane. Aiming to please, they submit safe, dull essays that invariably fall flat in the admissions office.

Hoping to inspire more potent writing, some colleges encourage applicants to "enjoy the experience" and claim to "look forward to reading your work and getting to know you a little bit better." Oberlin College recently told applicants, "Don't be afraid to take a risk, be original, to tell us about successful or not-so-successful experiences." Similarly, applicants to the University of Chicago are told to address topics "with utter seriousness, complete fancy, or something in between." Further instructions say, "Play, analyze (don't agonize), create, compose—let us hear the result of your thinking about something that interests you, in a voice that is your own."

Humor in Your Essay

Although essays that contain gimmicks, like puns, coined words, slang, and fractured English, may attract attention among thousands of ordinary essays, your attempt to be clever may tarnish your application. An ill-timed wisecrack could miss the funny bone of a weary admissions dean. This doesn't mean you should avoid humor. On the contrary: since you have plenty of opportunity to be sober and serious in the rest of the application, in the essay you can give your wit a workout. Readers will relish something playful, satirical, or whimsical. Don't overdo it, though. Tread lightly and cautiously with jokes and sarcasm.

> In your essay you can give your wit a workout.

What you and your friends may think is uproarious in the school lunchroom could fall on its face in the admissions office. In an essay submitted to Northwestern, a student joked that he would kill himself if he was rejected. "That wasn't funny," said a staffer in the admissions office. "The applicant didn't understand the concept of boundaries—of what is and isn't acceptable." Therefore, test your humor on an impartial adult before you send it to a college. If you're not usually a funny person, don't try to become one on your application. David Lettermans are not made overnight.

Sometimes gentle, self-effacing humor is best. No one at Harvard, for example, objected to Lisa E's tongue-in-cheek account of why she no longer dreamed of becoming an Amazon explorer:

> I would not make a very good adventurer for two reasons: motion sickness and ignorance. I am particularly prone to seasickness—an unfortunate circumstance, since the proper way

for adventurers to travel is in boats, preferably shipwrecked ones. As for ignorance, I am prone to ignorance in all areas; although in this case I am referring only to my ignorance of jungle survival tactics. I would undoubtedly perish within twenty-four hours of my arrival in the Amazon by drowning in a bog, treading on a sleeping snake, or ingesting a poisonous species of mushroom or grub. Then again, I might be stricken by some dread jungle malady or consumed for brunch by the very tribe of cannibals I had intended to study. Even worse, I might finally arrive in the Amazon only to find myself accosted by vendors of tribal nose rings and "I survived the Amazon" tee shirts.

In writing about a time when he experienced failure, Joel B, applying for the University of Pennsylvania, poked fun at his own ineptness as an outfielder in a childhood baseball game:

The game begins. Joel stolidly assumes his usual position in right field. Anxiety dominates his emotions. He is forced to stand outside on a field on a hot and sticky day, surrounded by clouds of swarming gnats. He fears that a ball may never be hit to him, and the only thing more fearful than that would be for a ball to be hit to him. His pet peeve on the baseball diamond is the "easy" pop fly. Joel wishes that people wouldn't include the word easy every time that phrase is used. He could be back in school demonstrating his academic prowess. Yes, school is a place where little Joel could shine! No one could hold a candle to his mastery of multiplication tables. Not to mention spelling. *There* is a field in which he could compete with the best of them.

In Sabrina E's essay for the University of Chicago you also find humor, but humor with a bite:

Before I arrived in my present high school, I attended school in Ireland. There are many differences between American and Irish education, not the least of which is the priority placed on actual teaching. Though in America scholarship comes first, in Ireland more time is spent trying to keep us on the paths of virtue than in steering us toward the paths of wisdom. Indeed, it seemed that a veritable legion of nuns was employed solely to safeguard our morals.

Whenever one of our regular teachers was absent, we were treated to one of Sister Assumpta's lectures. This latter-day saint was, by her own account, in direct communication with God. Apparently, each night as she prepared for bed, she would fall into a trance and converse with Him. This meant that whatever she told us came directly from the horse's mouth, although we were more inclined to believe that it came from the opposite end of the same animal.

Knowing that her irreverence might disqualify her at some colleges, Sabrina sent the essay anyway. She took a gamble, but for her it was worth it, since she wouldn't have wanted to attend a college where her humor wasn't appreciated.

As you begin to think about how you'll present yourself, keep asking two key questions: What's unique about me, and what do I want my reader to think of me? In your answers you're sure to find the seed of an essay that will work.

Reading Your Essay

Like customers, readers are always right. Maybe you won't like what they think about your essay. Maybe they'll misunderstand your intentions. They're still right. They get what they get—it's that simple.

Even the best writers can't always predict how readers will respond to their work. That's why you should plan to show your application essay to an unbiased reader or two before you submit it to a college. Ask your readers to tell you their impressions of the writer. If their impressions coincide with what you've intended, you're likely to have written a successful essay.

Remember that a real human being will be reading your essay. Therefore, write it as though you are addressing a sympathetic, receptive person—a friend, family member, or teacher. By keeping your audience in mind, you're bound to use language that is more personal and interesting.

In the pages that follow, you'll be privy to thoughts and reactions of a college admissions officer recorded alongside the text of four essays. Then you'll find a statement that summarizes each candidate's work.

(*Note*: Because admissions officials often find themselves inundated with applications, they rarely make comprehensive marginal notes. Rather, a brief summary statement is all they can manage. In the following essays, however, notes are included to better illustrate matters that essay readers think about as they evaluate essays.)

Joyce B

If someone were to ask me to describe myself, I would have to say that I am a person of many interests. I enjoy a simple life, yet I am not afraid to try new things.

Fairly dull opening. Hope it gets better. Essay has three parts; many interests, simple life, and new things. One topic, in depth, would probably be better.

I have been fortunate enough to become exposed to a variety of life-styles at a very early age. During my travels to Europe I was able to visit Germany, Italy, and Switzerland. There, I learned about different cultures and how other people live. Watching and meeting people is one of the many things that I enjoy.

"exposed"? Did she live the lifestyles or just observe them? "early age"? Three? Four? Ten? I wonder what she means. What could she have learned at age three?

Since the age of four, I have been dancing with "Dance Capri," a countywide Italian-American folk-dancing group. My involvement in this organization has introduced me to people who are interested in some of the same things I am. We enjoy learning about our Italian heritage and pride ourselves in keeping up the folk-dancing tradition.

No more travels? Now she's into dancing. How often does she dance? A major pastime?

Ah! She likes to join groups. That's good. I wonder if she speaks Italian.

Along with dancing, traveling, and meeting new people, I enjoy skiing and gymnastics. I usually ski in Vermont during my vacations, but last year I had the opportunity to ski in Quebec, Canada, for a week. I have always been on gymnastics teams, during the school year and the summer, and although I never won any special honors, I enjoy competitive gymnastics meets, especially the balance beam. For me, competing with a team has taught me what working for one common cause and reaching one common goal are like.

Good transition. But she's switched her focus again!

Not another topic! Athletics. Well, we can use her on the gymnastics team.

Not much new here. Pretty trite. An example could make this sound more honest.

One of the most relaxing hobbies I enjoy is cooking. When time permits, I bake and I prepare special meals for my family. I learned how to cook through various cooking courses that I took when I was younger. In high school, I could only fit one food preparation class into my program.

Along with this class, I enjoyed a variety of other courses in high school. However, the ones I liked the most were jewelry, Italian and history. I believe, though, that I made the most out of every course I took in high school.

Out of school, I invest a good deal of time in various part-time jobs. My work experience includes cashier and hostess work in an Italian restaurant, and my present job, which is working as a Gal Friday in an insurance office. I also baby-sit when I have the time.

High school was and still is a time of growing and maturing for me. Although working hard and getting good grades has always been my first priority, I also established and set many of the values that guide my life today. I can confidently say that in my senior year of high school I am ready to meet the challenges of college. I am ready to move on, and I see a bright future ahead of me.

Marginal notes:

Why were the courses special? Good grades? She seems diligent. I bet her teachers and counselors say she's a plugger.

She's been busy, all right. How much time could she have given to these jobs? I better check her list of work experiences.

What values?

Upbeat ending. But "youth faces tomorrow" isn't too interesting.

Note to Admissions Committee: Joyce B's essay suggests an active, but fragmented life. Joyce skids breezily from topic to topic, suggesting just casual involvement in many areas. Yes, she's well rounded, but so are most of our applicants. I can't find anything to distinguish her from others. After reading her essay, I don't know her very well.

Her writing is essentially correct, but it's boring. Not one of her paragraphs is developed beyond presenting some general facts about herself. Too much of her essay reiterates information already stated in her application. Moreover, Joyce fails to deliver what she promises in her opening passage. Where, for one, is her "simple life?" I recommend "rejection" unless there's substantial evidence in her file that contradicts my impression.

Chandra B

This is the fourth essay I'm writing, and it won't be any easier than any of the first three. You see, it isn't that I enjoy writing these essays, but with each one I have found out a little bit more about myself, and that is important to me. The purpose of each essay, of course, is to show that I have a sense of who I am, but there is always more to be found at the bottom of the well called "me." I wouldn't be fooling you or anyone if I said I know absolutely, totally everything there is to know about me.

My mother said to me this evening, as she finished reading my third essay, "You know what theme I find recurrent in each of these, Chandra? A sense of struggle, of some sort of tension within you. And that, I think, is what drives you. It is helping you in your maturation. Perhaps it needs resolving, but at the same time you know it is there, and you are dealing with it."

I think that for everyone sooner or later there is a time of inner tension and struggle—a time when one asks, "Who am I? What do I mean to myself?" It is those who face this struggle and deal with it rather than deny it, who eventually succeed in being who they want to be. One must learn to make choices about what one wants to stand for, to do with one's life, and at the same time one must learn to change oneself in order to achieve this.

My first essay dealt with a struggle in choosing between a German heritage and a Jewish one. My choice, however, was neither one nor the other, but a compromise to accept both as being part of me, to reconcile rather than to deny. My second essay dealt with a choice I may still have to make, namely between choosing marine biology or genetics as a career. This is a choice I may never have to make, for I may discover something I want to do more than either of them. I have not limited myself to only these two choices. Yet even now, I think I would decide upon marine biology, not because I find it more interesting, for I find

Hmmm, a common topic—the struggle of writing an essay.

Well, this is different: The struggle has been worth it. She's learned about herself. I wonder what she's learned?

Perceptive. A good idea! We can't know ourselves completely, can we?

Hmm, a sensitive mother, but c'mon, no mother talks like that. She sounds like a psychology text. Good point, though, and the dialogue adds life.

Vague paragraph. A bit ponderous. I wonder what she's driving at.

Now I see! She's been struggling for an identity. And it hasn't been easy. Her mother was right.

Struggle to communicate? That's splendid! Chandra's a deep thinker.

them both equally so, but because I enjoy it more; I have more fun with it. My third essay dealt with a struggle I will always face, namely my need to communicate. I feel the need to know about others, and to have others learn about me. This is my way of sharing myself and partaking in others. My struggle is a fight against misunderstanding and loneliness. When we communicate, whether between people or nations, we understand each other. When we communicate, we bridge the gap of loneliness.

She seems high-strung, a little tense. Is that why she's lonely? I wonder what her teachers say.

Ah, she's come back to the struggle again. Conclusion recalls her opening. Nice way to unify the piece.

There will always be struggles within me, dilemmas I will face. I am determined to resolve these tensions. With each choice, I choose who I am, who I will become. Most importantly, though, it is I who makes these choices, not someone else. That is what self-determination is all about.

She's convinced me. I believe she'll win her struggle. Strong, up-beat ending.

Note to Admissions Committee:

Chandra B views life as a serious undertaking. Her writing has conviction. She's not going to play her way through college or engage in foolishness. Her thoughtful—nay, philosophical—ideas attest to her maturity. She probably drives herself hard, maybe compulsively. She seems genuinely bound on a quest to find an identity.

Will she study hard in college? You bet, and will probably get A's. Will she contribute to the college? Intellectually, yes, and maybe in other ways, too. Let's accept her and several more passionate thinkers like her. I hope that her teacher and counselor recommendations confirm my impression that Chandra is a rare find.

Angela C

As far back as I can remember, I have excelled at sports. I was always the first in my kindergarten class to reach the swings during recess and the first to climb to the top of the rope during gym. However, while most six-year-old girl athletes tend to develop into "school-yard jocks," I seemed to lack that aggressive, competitive nature. I was much more content reading my book than keeping up with the boys. By the time I entered high school, I was clearly defined as a "student," not a "jock."

When I tried out for the field hockey team in ninth grade, it was merely because a good friend of mine begged me to do it with her. The idea of spending three hours every day running around a field didn't particularly appeal to me, but for a friend I'd do anything. After two weeks, my friend quit. Quitting has always been anathema to me, but in this case it never entered my mind anyway. I was having fun. Those three hours of practice were the best part of my day. I loved being outside, and being physically active. Most importantly, I loved being with my teammates. Between studying and practicing the piano, I'd spend so much time alone that my time on the field became a welcome and necessary break in my day. Also, coming home at six o'clock every evening helped me to budget my time, since I knew I only had a few hours in which to complete my assignments.

It wasn't until my sophomore year that field hockey became more important to me than just a social activity. It was still terrific fun since I loved getting to know the juniors and seniors on the team whom otherwise I would never have met. Some of them are still my closest friends. However, playing on the varsity squad was a very different experience from playing on the freshman team. I found myself missing holidays and giving up weekends to play hockey. The team now required a serious dedication and commitment, which I was willing to make since I enjoyed it so much. As my commitment became more serious, so did my attitude toward field hockey. I realized that I couldn't accept being a mediocre player.

Starts off like just another "jock" essay—but very graceful. An appealing opening.

Oh, she's not a jock, after all. Smooth shift from kindergarten to ninth grade.

Well, she's a student and an athlete.

A rich paragraph! Shows Angela's loyalty to friends. Her perseverance, too. And the fun she's had.

And she has other interests, too.

She's well organized. That shows in her essay.

Good transition. This is moving right along. Angela is a serious hockey player.

She's obviously committed to the sport. Good, detailed writing.

She's a hard driver, too.

Interesting! She took on a challenge and won, and she's proud of her achievement. A good point.

Effective conclusion. She's summarizing her career and showing how she's changed. Good writing. How successful she's been! And modest, too.

What determination! I think she'll make it. She's unstoppable.

Mediocre is one of the most negative words I know. I knew in my sophomore year that, as the new player on the varsity team, I was also an average player. Traveling to Holland with my field hockey team revealed to me again my inadequacies when I saw the skill of some of the Europeans. Since then, by attending camps and clinics and playing in summer leagues, I've really worked hard to become a good player. I always want to be good—if not the best—at everything to which I set my mind. To be a good student comes naturally to me, but for me to be a good field hockey player requires work.

I remember when I first started playing field hockey. I thought that to be an all-county player and captain of the varsity was to be the best. Well, I *am* an all-county player and I *am* the captain of the team but one thing I am certainly not, is the best. Whenever I achieve one of my many goals, it always seems as if a new one appears ahead of me. Now that I'm a good high school player, I'm ready to start at the bottom again and work to become a good college player.

Note to Admissions Committee:

Angela C clearly demonstrates self-confidence and an upbeat personality. She's good at everything, and she enjoys all she does. Her essay indicates that she's loyal, well-organized, determined, committed to success, industrious, and fun-loving. Yet, she doesn't bowl you over with her attributes. Instead, she casually tosses them into the story of her growth as a field hockey player. In spite of all her virtues, she neither brags nor sounds like a Boy Scout. She's an all-round scholar-athlete.

Angela can write! There's not an ill-chosen word or awkward phrase in the piece. Could she have received help? Look for confirmation of writing talent in her grades and references.

My recommendation: If she's really as good as she sounds, offer her the dean's house and a Ferrari!

Eric H

It is Friday afternoon, a time I can so vividly remember enjoying. School would let out, and no matter how much homework I had, I could always relax Friday and Saturday. Unfortunately, T.G.I.F. has evolved into O.S.I.F. (Oh @#$%, it's Friday!).

A catchy opening.

Joint custody: an American revolution. Friday is the transition day, the day that a week's worth of subsistence materials have to be transported from one parent's abode to the other's. My room at Dad's has to be cleaned, my clothes washed and pressed, and other essentials placed in order. Then my odyssey commences. Somehow, I have to get all of my belongings from one end of town to the other.

Oh, another essay on divorce.

"subsistence materials" Ugh! Does he mean toothpaste, underwear, a week's supply of socks?"

"abode," "commences" Too fancy.

Usually, Mom picks me up. She tries to be tolerant but at times loses her cool. "I'm only going to do this once. If you forget anything, that's your tough luck." I try to explain that I can't fit everything I own into her Toyota. Sometimes she forgets that I didn't ask for this asinine way of life. In any event, four trips to the car later, we leave home and head for home.

Mother sounds like an ogre, probably the villain in this story.

"asinine" Good word. Eric sounds bitter.

Ah, a good line. Sardonic humor.

By the time I'm really settled, another week has passed. O.S.I.F.!, and I find myself out of breath exactly where I started. In the span of two weeks I have accomplished nothing except total aggravation. I can't even blink for fear that another Friday will come.

I don't get the point of all this. Does he mean that his life is a treadmill? Why doesn't he say so?

Like anything else, joint custody has its bright side. When my parents were divorced, Dad had a big decision to make: pack up and forget his little brats or remain for the duration. Even though he's never been nominated for any Best Daddy awards, he hasn't regretted his decision to stay.

Ah, good. There's a bright side to the story.

Well, Dad's no hero either.

The entire ordeal has brought us a world closer. When we were quite suddenly hurled into an unamiable apartment without Mom, we shared a common interest: survival. Neither of us knew how to break an egg, sew a hem, or clean a toilet bowl.

Shows maturity and responsibility, I guess.

Sixty dollars? Only sixty dollars? that's hard to swallow!

Puzzling. Didn't he grow close to his father? Something's missing here.

Well, good. He can make jokes, despite his misery.

Who suggested?

Well stated

Cute ending.

He refused to learn these things, so I had to. Today, six years later, I cook all the meals, do all the shopping, and make most of the household decisions in place of my father. He basically grants me a generous expense account of sixty dollars on Friday night, and it is up to me to see that food is purchased for the week. This burden has done wonders for my character. Many of my friends fear life at college, but not I. If I can tolerate life with my father, campus life will undoubtedly be a breeze.

Another advantage to joint custody is variety. Just when I get sick of the accumulated dishes, dirty laundry, and ravenous cockroaches that are a way of life at my Dad's, I can run to Mom's for a week. Come the next Friday, you can be sure that I'll be so fed up with my mother's vexatious organization and fetish for punctuality that I'll welcome cockroaches with open arms. I think that's what is meant by escapism.

It has been suggested that I stop writing essays complaining about joint custody and simply leave half of my stuff at either house. It seems logical. Maybe that's the problem; it makes sense. I don't think divorce and custody were destined by the Almighty to make sense. I suppose I just have some psychological aversion to leaving fifty percent of my life unattended for a week.

All in all, I suppose joint custody isn't so bad. I'm never bored, and I'm always on my toes. Oh @#$%, I've got to run. It's Friday!

Note to Admissions Committee:

Eric H certainly has courage! He took a personal gamble by writing about an obviously painful subject. It's not that he's looking for sympathy, but rather he chose to vent his anger about being shuttled between his parents each week. He has a right to be bitter, but I question his judgment in using the application essay as a place to blow off steam.

The essay is meant to be humorous, and it is— to a point. The humor is a thin disguise, though, for someone who laughs to hide his tears. My guess is that Eric's anguish makes him hard to like, but I'd like to know what his counselor and teachers think.

He's not a bad writer, but he seems to flaunt his vocabulary—not always successfully—perhaps thinking that college people will be impressed. His work lacks polish, but I think that in time it will improve.

His essay works neither for nor against his candidacy. My recommendation will be based on the other information in his application and file.

4 COMPOSING YOUR ESSAY

You probably won't get out of high school without writing some sort of essay on *Macbeth,* or if not *Macbeth,* then on the Great Depression or protein synthesis. By this time in your life, in fact, you've probably written enough essays to fill a large book. When writing those essays, perhaps you sat down, spilled your thoughts onto the computer screen, printed it out, and handed in your paper. Maybe you wrote a rough draft and went back later to rephrase and cut and paste your ideas. Possibly, you thought out ahead of time what you wanted to say and prepared a list of ideas or an outline. Maybe you used a combination of methods, varying them from time to time according to the importance of the essay.

Everyone who writes uses a process of some kind. Some processes seem to work better than others. The variations are endless, however, and the actual process you use is as personal and unique as your fingerprints. Since it is personal, let me step out of my role as writing instructor for a moment and describe the process I used to write this chapter so far.

Before I even turned my computer on, I had a general idea of what I wanted to say: namely, that anyone facing an essay question on a college application has already had plenty of writing experience and that the same process a person used to write essays in school can be used to write an essay for college. Furthermore, I wanted to assure the reader that no single process is better than any other, as long as it works. With those thoughts floating around in my head, I started to write, hoping that one idea would flow smoothly into the next. I also hoped that extraneous ideas wouldn't lead me away from what I had in mind, something that frequently happens when I write.

> The process you use to write is as personal and unique as your fingerprints.

Fairly rapidly for me, because I'm usually a very slow writer, I typed the first two paragraphs. Then I reread them. Luckily, they seemed to stick to the topic and they more or less expressed my thoughts. I wasn't altogether happy with my opening sentence, however, which originally read, "By this time in your life you must have written a ream of essays." I thought that some of my readers wouldn't know the word *ream,* so I changed the sentence to one that would surely evoke an image of a lot of pages: "By this time in your life you must have written enough essays to fill a large book."

A moment later, however, I decided that even that sentence wasn't right for an opening. I needed an idea that hit closer to my readers' experience. So I inserted two new sentences, turning my original first sentence into the third. Still later, I added the phrase "in fact" to that sentence, intending to bind the thoughts in the first three sentences more closely to each other.

As you see, I like to write a few paragraphs as quickly as I can, then return to them before going on. I don't always do that, however. Sometimes I write more, sometimes less, before doubling back to rewrite and edit. Other writers work differently, and so, no doubt, do you.

If you compare my original opening paragraphs, reproduced below, with the printed version at the start of this chapter, you'll discover several more changes, each intended to make the writing clearer and more interesting. All the while, I kept thinking of you, my reader. I figured that if you are going to spend time reading my words, the least I could do is make the time worth your while. I also wanted to make you feel compelled to read on. If your cell phone rang while you were reading, I was hoping you'd be annoyed at the interruption.

> By this time in your life you must have written a ream of essays. In fourth grade, remember writing about "My Trip to Disney World"? More recently, perhaps, you wrote about irony in *Macbeth* or Chinese immigration to the United States. When you wrote those essays, you probably used a technique that seemed right for you. Perhaps you just sat down, spilled your thoughts onto the page, went back later, and reorganized and rephrased your ideas over and over. You may have thought out what you wanted to say ahead of time and prepared some sort of list or outline of your ideas to guide you as you wrote. You may have used a combination of methods.

> Everyone who writes anything uses a process of some kind. Some processes seem to work better than others for certain writers. The variations are endless, however, and the actual process you use is personal and as unique to you as your fingerprints. Since it is so personal, let me step down from my post as giver of information about essay writing for a moment and describe the process I used to write this chapter so far.

Thinking About Your Reader

You and I have made a kind of agreement. Simply by reading these words, you have agreed to let me enter your life. Thanks. My end of the bargain is harder. I have to keep writing until I'm finished, but you can stop reading at any time.

I don't want you to stop, however. So as I write, I try everything I can to hold your interest, to keep your mind and eyes fastened to these words. That's a tough assignment. Since you're a stranger to me, I don't know what you'll understand or what will grab you. I have to keep guessing. Even if my guess is wrong, I can't stop, can't go back and try again. If you shut this book right now, I'll never know it. No physical force in the universe is strong enough to keep one small muscle in your head from shifting your eyes away from this page. Only the compelling power of my words, along with some lucky guesswork, can do it.

As a writer of a college essay, you face a challenge similar to mine, except that you can be pretty sure your reader will stick with you to the last word. Because you have a reasonable guarantee of an audience doesn't make the job of writing any easier, however. You're still obliged to give the readers something they want to read. Writing the essay is a lot like giving a gift to a friend. You think about what your friend would like, you try to please, you choose carefully and you present the gift as stylishly as you can. If all goes well, you get a reward for your effort.

> Writing an essay is a lot like giving a gift to a friend. You try to please.

But, first, it's work.

Warming Up

Once you've read the possible essay topics, you're likely to start thinking about what to write. As you reach into your background to search for a subject, don't lose heart if at first you come up empty-handed. You may need a warming-up period to help you find a subject and to prime you for the vigorous mental work ahead. In fact, the ultimate quality of your essay may depend in part on your warm-ups.

For most students, the high school years rush by like a raging river. It's hard to stop and step back a moment to reflect on your life, on how far you've come and where you'd like to go. Now, on the verge of applying to college, is the right time for you to try.

Start with a personal inventory. The key word is *personal*—for your eyes only. Think of who you are and how you got that way. You might begin, for example, simply by making a list of adjectives that describe what you like about yourself. Then make another list of what you dislike. Don't worry if the second list is longer than the first—most people are pretty hard on themselves. Study these lists for patterns, inconsistencies, and unusual combinations. For instance, Gina S, whose list appears below, considers herself both "generous to others" and "self-centered." Is Gina contradicting herself? Is she being untruthful? Does she change from time to time? Since the list is personal, no one but Gina needs to know.

Gina's Personal Inventory

What I like about myself	*What I dislike*
loyal to my friends	my nose
idealistic	short temper
trusting	uncomfortable with
prompt in replying to	strangers
instant messages	need a lot of sleep
determined to succeed	addicted to my iPhone
mysterious	impulsive
ambitious	lack of athletic talent
competitive	can't carry a tune
generous to others	gluttonish
insightful about myself	envious of friends
sensitive to others' feelings	(sometimes)
good listener	overconsiderate of
good memory	others (sometimes)
energetic	math and heavy metal
flirtatious	often late for
skillful as a blogger	appointments
great smile	self-centered
	stubborn
	basically shy
	indecisive

Once you complete a list, rank the qualities in order of importance. Which quality would you be most reluctant to give up? Which would you give up first? Which are you proudest of? Which would you most like to change? A compilation of answers to such questions identify your interests and, to a degree, define your values and describe your personality.

Most items on your own personal inventory will differ from Gina's. Yet, it shouldn't surprise you to find some similarities. Although no item may immediately strike you as the focus of a distinctive essay, a few imaginative connections could lead you directly to a suitable subject. Notice how Gina might have developed several possible subjects from her inventory:

> Gina claims to be "competitive," but she also "lacks athletic talent." Her competitive nature, therefore, may emerge in the classroom instead of the gym. Perhaps she competes to win awards as the best reader, writer or mathematician. She may compete for recognition on the job or at home. Regardless of the place, Gina's need to excel could be the focus of her essay.
>
> Gina says she's a "glutton," presumably for food. Since a college doesn't necessarily need to know that, Gina could turn gluttony into a metaphor and focus her essay on being a glutton for success. Perhaps she derives satisfaction from being a successful student, friend or member of a particular group.
>
> Gina also says she's "impulsive." In a way, her "short temper" confirms that she occasionally rushes into things. On the other hand, she might point out that her impulsiveness gives her an urge to help anyone in need. Her essay might focus on an incident that demonstrates her unusual generosity. A brief discussion about becoming a social worker someday would add a fitting conclusion to her essay.

Ultimately, Gina found her subject in an incident that would not have occurred unless she truly had a "good memory." This excerpt from her essay tells what happened:

> I had just come from the elephant house at the zoo when I spotted Bucky, my old swimming counselor at Camp Merriwood. It was six years since I saw him last. I remembered him only in a Princeton tee shirt and a swimsuit and

never imagined that he even owned long pants and a parka, but I recognized his face instantly. I called out his name and introduced myself.

He looked at me and said, "Oh, I remember you, Gina," but I knew he was just being polite. To him I could have been Jenny, Margie, Eva, Ruthie, Lilah, Lucy, or any one of the dozens of squealing ten-year-old girls at camp that summer.

We talked a little while about people and events at camp. No, he didn't really remember the kids on my relay team. Well yes, he only had a faint memory of the swim meet we won against Camp Harding, in which I won two races.

"What are you up to now?" he asked. When I told him I was looking for a summer job, he said his company sometimes hired high school students in the summer and that I should apply.

Gina landed a summer job in Bucky's firm doing something called "customer relations," a glamorous term for helping to keep the files straight. Gina observed in her essay, though, that she was glad to be working at all. Then she added:

I got the job as a result of having a good memory. Since then I have become more interested in memory and how it works. I have read some books on the subject and have learned some ways to improve my own memory. In less than a minute I can now memorize ten vocabulary words or the names of ten people I never met before. Elephants are not supposed to forget, which may or may not be true. However, I wonder if remembering Bucky was related to my visit to the elephants in the zoo.

Gina launched her essay with a short anecdote meant to illustrate her good memory. For every quality you list on a personal inventory, try also to think of evidence that proves that you are indeed what you claim to be. A single example is all it takes to get an essay underway.

Another place to locate essay subjects is in your answers to a set of questions such as these:

—What are you good at?
—What are you trying to get better at?

—What has been your greatest success? Your greatest failure?

—What three words would you like engraved on your tombstone?

—What is your strongest conviction? Would you die for it?

—What would you do with a million dollars?

—If the world were to end a year from today, how would you spend your remaining time?

Thoughtful answers to often whimsical questions may trigger any number of essay possibilities. As you toss ideas back and forth in your head, keep your distance from stock responses— those that will lump you with the crowd. Walk around for a few days letting yourself think about what makes you unique. Tell someone what's on your mind. Keep a notebook in your pocket, because a great thought may hit you at any time. Keep pen and pad by your bed to record a four-in-the-morning inspiration. Do some free-writing. Think hard about what you want your readers to think of you. In short, do something to jump-start your writing muscles.

Some people call this part of the process "prewriting." You might call it getting yourself "psyched." Whatever the name, it's the time you spend messing with possibilities and tuning up to write. It may even include finding a quiet, uncluttered place to work without distractions. It involves laying aside many hours of time for solitary, unhurried work.

> Prewriting may include finding a quiet place for hours of solitary, unhurried work.

Warm-up time should also include a search for the point, or focus, of your essay. Identifying a subject isn't enough. Now you must focus on what you'll say about the subject. The sharper your focus, the better. You can't expect to include everything in a 250- to 500-word essay.

Maybe the surest way to narrow your subject is to begin writing. If your essay seems dull and disappointing after a couple of paragraphs, you're probably being too vague, too impersonal, or both. Keep going, for you may discover the point of your essay at any time. Be prepared, however, to recognize that you may occasionally write yourself into a dead end. Not every subject works. If you find yourself blocked on all sides, you have no choice but to grit your teeth, turn to another topic, and start over.

If you end up dry, even after several attempts, you might try this twenty-question technique for unlocking ideas. Write your subject at the top of a page. Then ask twenty questions about the subject, leaving plenty of space for writing answers. Linda W, for example, knew she wanted to write an essay on dancing, but she didn't know what to say about it. At first she wrote, "During the last eight years dancing has provided me with great satisfaction." Because every devoted ballerina feels exactly the same way, however, Linda quickly realized that her idea was b-o-r-ing. So Linda started asking and answering questions like these:

What kind of dancing do I like the most?

When did I first fall in love with dancing?

Why doesn't everybody dance?

What would my life be like without dancing?

Who has been important to me in my dancing? Why?

If I could not dance, what art form would I use to express myself?

What am I giving up or sacrificing by devoting so much time to dance?

How good a dancer am I? How can I find out?

The first questions were easy. When the questions grew hard, both to ask and to answer, Linda had begun to dig deeply into her topic. In figuring out answers, she finally discovered an original point to make in her essay:

To me, dancing is the most dynamic and personal of the arts. Pictures and sculptures are displayed in museums. Poems and stories are hidden in books. To make music you play someone else's notes on an instrument made by another person. But dancing, ah, dancing, is like life itself.

Where Linda crossed over from prewriting to actually composing her first draft is hard to say, nor is it critical to know. What counts is that she found a topic, narrowed its focus, and stated a compelling thesis for an essay.

Writing the Essay

By the time some writers begin to compose their essays they more or less know that they'll reach their destination using the famous five-paragraph essay formula. Other writers will start more tentatively, knowing their general direction but not finding the specific route until they get there.

Neither method is better than the other, for much depends on the subject matter and intent of the writer. The first method follows a simple, clear-cut formula, which may not win a prize for originality but can help to turn a muddle of ideas into a model of clarity. It has a beginning, a middle, and an end.

The *formula* is simply an all-purpose plan for arranging ideas into a clear, easy-to-follow order. You have probably used it in school for answering a test question, analyzing a poem or reporting lab work. You can call on it anytime you need to set ideas in order. Its greatest virtue is clarity. Each part has its place and purpose.

The formula

Introduction

Body
$\begin{cases} \text{Point 1} \\ \text{Point 2} \\ \text{Point 3} \end{cases}$

Conclusion

In reality, however, writers rarely follow the *formula*. In fact, you may never see a formula essay in print. Yet a majority of college essays, even those that take circuitous paths between the beginning and end, adhere to some sort of three-step organization. In the *introduction,* writers lay out their plans for the essay. In the *body* they develop their ideas, and in the *conclusion* they leave the reader with a thought to remember. Since all writers differ, however, you find endless variations within each step, as you're about to see.

Introductions: Hooking the Reader

Use the introduction to let readers know what they're in for. Don't, however, make a formal announcement of your plan: "This essay is about my community-service work last summer." Just state your point. The reader will recognize the topic soon enough, even without a separate statement of your intention. Maria G, for example, began her essay this way: "Working for two months in Mother Theresa's Soup Kitchen on the lower East Side with the St. Augustine Teen Club has changed my life." This opening promises the reader an account of Maria's work in the slums and what the experience has meant to her. It also sets the essay's boundaries. Maria can't include everything about dismal conditions in lower Manhattan. Instead, she'll concentrate on her own experience there, and no more.

The best essays usually begin with something catchy, something to lure the reader into the piece. Basically, it's a hook—a phrase, sentence, or idea that will grab readers' interest so completely that they'll keep on reading almost in spite of themselves. Once you've hooked your readers, you can lead them anywhere.

> The best essays begin with a "hook" to catch the reader's interest.

Hooks must be very sharp, very clean. They must surprise, inform, or tickle the reader in an instant. A dull hook just won't do. Here are a few samples of each:

DULL HOOK

My difficulty in dealing with my feelings probably all started when my parents' marriage started breaking up.

SHARPER HOOK

The first thing I remember is my parents arguing in the next room while I was trying to sleep.

The sharper hook is vivid. It creates a compelling image of a child in the dark, attempting to block out the sounds of his parents' shouting. It also provokes curiosity. The reader wants to know more.

DULL HOOK

The book, *Divine Comedy*, is a serious work of literature, written by Dante several centuries ago.

SHARPER HOOK

Dante's *Divine Comedy*, despite its title, is not a funny book.

The second hook contains a small surprise for the reader. No one who knows Dante's work about the author's travels through Hell, would think of it as humorous. Yet, a student coming to the title for the first time might expect to be amused. The mistake is worth a chuckle—but only if you're familiar with the book.

DULL HOOK

Among my various extracurricular commitments, music has been the most enduring.

SHARPER HOOK

I have tried to immerse myself in music.

In the sharper hook, the terse declaration of the writer's commitment to music makes the point quickly. As the reader, you know instantly that music is the topic. Moreover, the repetition of the "m" sound has a certain appeal.

Naturally, your essay's opening ought to be appropriate to your topic and tone. A serious discussion of Mother Theresa's Soup Kitchen probably shouldn't begin with an irreverent story about a nun. Beware also of any introduction that's too cute or precious. Be thoughtful and clever, yes; obnoxious, no. If you quickly want to lure your reader into your essay, consider any of these five common methods:

> Your opening should be appropriate to your topic and tone.

1. Start with an incident, real or invented, that leads the reader gracefully to the point of your essay.

   "How about 'John Henry' in A?"

The banjo player kicks off the tune with a solid lead and is joined by the other field pickers in a couple of seconds. Having sung the first verse and chorus, I strum along on the guitar and let my mind wander. How incongruous for me, a product of upper-middle-class suburbia, to be standing in the middle of a grassy field picking bluegrass and old-timey music until dawn.

—Steve M

2. State a provocative idea in an ordinary way or an ordinary idea in a provocative way. Either will spark the reader's interest.

If you've never been six feet seven inches tall like me, you probably don't know what it's like up here. Everybody is a comedian when they meet you. They call you "Beanpole," or ask, "How's the weather up there?" or tell you to "Watch out for low-flying planes!" Not only that, they expect you to play basketball, have bumps on your head from doorways, and know things that shorties don't.

—Andy S

3. Use a quotation—not necessarily a famous one. Shakespeare's or your grandmother's will do, as long as it relates to the topic of your essay.

True ease in writing comes from art, not chance,
as those move easiest who have learn'd to dance.
—Alexander Pope,
An Essay on Criticism

It took me eight years to understand Pope's message. I know now that he should have said, "True ease in dance comes from wonderful, frustrating, exciting, tedious, time-consuming, strenuous, and sweaty work, not chance." That may not sound as good, but it's as true.

—Lisa B

4. Knock down a commonly held assumption or define a word in a new and surprising way.

No doubt you've heard that Latin is a dead language. Wrong! Latin is alive and well and living inside my head, thanks to a wonderful teacher who emphasized the culture, not the conjugations, in the language.

—Alicia G

5. Ask an interesting question or two, which you will answer in your essay.

> "Tell me, in God's name, why you, Terry D, want to become an English teacher!"
>
> "Because . . . because I want to teach," I stammered. I bent my head, hoping my answers would satisfy him and defuse the unbearable tension that stalked about me.
>
> "Come, Terry, that's not the reason; there's more to it than what you've said. Now why do you want to teach? Is it the kids? The classroom? Power? What force within yourself causes you to associate English and teaching?"
>
> —Teresa D

In any collection of good essays you'd no doubt find other examples of catchy openings. Whatever your opening, however, it must fit your writing style and personality. Work hard at getting it right, but at the same time, not too hard. An opening that seems forced may irk your reader, and one that comprises, say, more than a quarter of your essay is way too long.

If you can't find a suitable opening when you begin to write your essay, don't put off writing the rest. As you write the body of the essay, a bright idea may hit you. Some writers begin by writing three paragraphs, fully expecting to throw away the first two. They need at least two paragraphs to hit their stride and to rid their minds of useless ideas. By the time they've reached paragraph three, they've figured out the point of their essays. Only then do they turn to writing a hook. You might try that. If your "throwaway" paragraphs contain ideas you can't live without, recycle them later in your essay.

The Body: Putting the Pieces Together

To build a house you must start on the ground. On your foundation you construct a frame, then add walls, a roof, a satellite dish and you're done! The builder must follow this order or the house will crumble.

Order is important to the writer, too. What should come first? Second? Third? In most writing the best order is the clearest order, the arrangement your reader can follow with the least effort.

Just as a highway map shows several routes from one town to another, there is no single way to get from the beginning of a piece of writing to the end. The route you take depends on the purpose of the trip. The order of ideas in the body of your essay will vary according to what you want to do to your reader. Whether you want to shock, sadden, inspire, inform, or entertain the reader, each purpose will have its own best order. In story-telling, the events are often placed in the sequence in which they occur. To explain a childhood memory or define who you are, to stand up for gay rights or describe a poignant moment— each may take some other particular arrangement. No one plan is superior to another, provided you have a valid reason for using it.

The plan that fails is the aimless one, the one in which ideas are arranged solely on the basis of the order in which they popped into your head. To guard against aimlessness, rank your ideas in order of importance either before you start or while you're writing drafts. Although your first idea may turn out to be your best, you probably should save it for later in your essay. Giving it away at the start is self-defeating. To hold your reader's interest, it's better to work toward your best point, not away from it. If you have, say, three good points to make, save your zinger for last. Launch your essay with your second best, and tuck your least favorite between the other two.

> To hold the reader's interest, work toward your best point, not away from it.

A body consisting of three sections may be just about right, although no hard-and-fast rule says so. Why *three*? Mainly because three is a number that seems to work. When you can make three statements about a subject, you probably know what you're talking about. One is too simple, and two is still pretty shallow, but three seems thoughtful. Psychologically, three also creates a sense of wholeness, like the beginning, middle, and end of a story. Each point doesn't necessarily receive equal treatment. You might manage one point with a single paragraph, but the others may get more. Each point has to be distinctive: Your third point mustn't be a rerun of the first or second.

It shouldn't be difficult to break the main point of most essays into at least three secondary points, regardless of their topic or form. A narrative essay, for example, naturally breaks into a beginning, middle, and end. A process is likely to have at least three steps, some of which may be broken into substeps. In an essay of comparison and contrast, you ought to be able to find at least three similarities and differences to write about. A similar division into thirds applies to essays of cause and effect, definition and description, and certainly to essays of argumentation.

Turn back to the sample essays in Chapter 3. Each of the successful pieces follows the three-part pattern. In rough outline, they look like this:

Chandra's essay (page 85)

Subject:	The struggles within me
Point 1:	What do I stand for?
Point 2:	What should I do with my life?
Point 3:	How can I communicate with others?

Angela's essay (page 87)

Subject:	My field hockey career
Point 1:	Starting out in ninth grade—a social activity
Point 2:	In tenth and eleventh grade—fun and dedication
Point 3:	Becoming a champion—a serious commitment

Eric's essay (page 89)

Subject:	Joint custody
Point 1:	Description of my weekly ordeal
Point 2:	My relationship with my mother and father
Point 3:	How joint custody has changed me

Only Joyce's essay (page 83) defies analysis into three sections. In fact, the piece fails for that very reason. Joyce tried to make more than half a dozen different points. Each point remains undeveloped, and in the end the essay is little more than a list of Joyce's interests and activities.

Transitions and Paragraphs: Taking Readers by the Hand

Readers need to be led. As you write, think of readers as tourists and your essay as a trip they take from one place to another. You are their guide, their travel agent.

After you've told them where they're going (the introduction), now and then remind them (in the body of the essay) where they're headed. In long essays readers need more reminders than in short ones. To keep readers well informed, you don't have to repeat what you've written, but rather plant key ideas, slightly rephrased, as milestones along the way. (The sentence you just read contains just such a marker. The phrase *"To keep a reader well informed"* prompts you to keep in mind the topic being discussed—that is, helping readers find their way.) Watch out for detours, for you may lose your readers if you step too far outside the path you laid out at the start. (The sentence you just read is a detour. Yes, it's related to the topic but it steers the discussion away from guiding readers through an essay.)

Also, help readers along by choosing words that set up relationships between one idea and the next. This can be done with such words as *this,* the very word that ties the sentence you are now reading to the previous one. The English language supplies numerous words and phrases for tying sentences and ideas together, among them:

also	on the other hand	still
too	consequently	another
further	therefore	finally
in addition	although	in the first place
similarly	moreover	regardless
as a result	nevertheless	on the contrary
however	now	better still
for instance	this	yet

Each time you link one sentence to another with a transitional word or phrase, you help readers through your writing. Without such help, or when every sentence stands unconnected to the next, readers may end up hopelessly lost, like travelers going down roads without signposts or markers.

Links between sentences lend a hand to writers, too. They help writers stick to the topic. Ideas that don't connect clearly with others should be moved or thrown out.

The inventor of the paragraph also figured out a simple way to mark the path through a piece of writing. The paragraph indentation is a signal to readers to get ready for a change in thought or idea, somewhat like the directional blinker telling other drivers that you're about to turn.

Yet not every new paragraph signals a drastic change. The writer may simply want to move the essay ahead one step at a time, and paragraphs illuminate each step.

Some paragraphs spring directly from those that came before. Like infants, they can't stand alone. The paragraph before this one, for example, is linked to the previous one by the connecting word *yet*. The connection has cued you to get ready for a contrasting thought, but it also reminded you that the two paragraphs are related.

Abrupt starts are best from time to time. Suddenness will surprise and keep readers alert. Connecting words will dilute the impact of the surprise. Be wary of a string of abrupt starts, however, because too many quick shifts may annoy more than surprise.

Paragraphs let your readers skip rapidly through your work, particularly when each first or last sentence summarizes the rest of the paragraph. Readers may then focus on paragraph openings and closings and skip what's in between. Readers in a hurry will appreciate that, but you can force readers to linger a while by varying the location of the most important idea in each paragraph.

Whether your readers skim your paragraphs or slog doggedly through every word, they need to find sentences now and then that, like landmarks, help them to know where they are. Such guiding sentences differ from others because they define the paragraph's main topic; hence the name *topic sentence*.

Most, but not all, paragraphs contain topic sentences. The topic of some paragraphs is so obvious that to state it would be redundant. Then, too, groups of paragraphs can be so closely knit that one topic sentence states the most important idea for all of them.

> Consider your readers absent-minded wanderers. Remind them often where they are.

No rule governs every possible use of a topic sentence. A sense of what readers need in order to understand your meaning must guide you. Consider your readers absent-minded wanderers. Since they tend to lose their way, remind them often about where they are. Let the topic sentences lead. If in doubt, grasp their hands too firmly rather than too loosely. Follow the principle that if there is any way to misunderstand or misinterpret your words, readers are bound to find it.

The Conclusion: Giving a Farewell Gift

When you reach the end of your essay, you can stop writing and be done with it. Or, you can present your reader with a little something to remember you by, a *gift*—an idea to think about, a line to chuckle over, a memorable phrase or quotation. Whatever you give, the farewell gift must fit the content, style, and mood of your essay.

> Send your readers off feeling glad that they stayed with you to the end.

Some writers think that endings are more important than beginnings. After all, by the time readers arrive at the conclusion, your introduction may have already begun to fade from memory.

Making a reference to the opening reminds readers of the essay's purpose. It also creates a sense of wholeness. A well-phrased ending will stick with readers and influence their feelings about your essay and, of course, about its writer. Therefore, choose a farewell gift thoughtfully. Be particular. Send your readers off feeling good or laughing, weeping, angry, thoughtful, or thankful, but above all, glad that they stayed with your essay to the end.

A conclusion that's too pat or common will leave readers with the impression that you were too cheap to give the best gift you could, or that you chose your gift in haste. Stay away especially from bargain-basement gifts like these:

> The failures I had in the past will help me in college and in the future. (from an essay on experiencing failure)

> Then I woke up and saw that it was all a dream. (from an essay about a place where you feel utterly content)

> I'd recommend this book to anyone who likes historical novels. (from an essay about a personal accomplishment—reading every word of *War and Peace*)

In conclusion, if I can be half as successful as my aunt, I will live happily every after. (from an essay about challenging a belief or idea)

Such trite endings suggest that the writers couldn't think of anything original to say or that they just wanted to get their essays over with. Either way, a stale conclusion can spoil a good essay.

Readers will appreciate almost any gift you give them, provided you've put some thought into your choice. When writing the ending, let your instinct guide you. You've read enough stories and plays and have heard enough songs to know what endings sound like, what lends a sense of completeness to a creative piece of work. For example, when you tell readers how an unresolved issue was settled, or when you speculate on what might occur in the future, readers sense that an ending is at hand.

Even commonly used endings can be turned into stylish gifts, as these samples show:

1. Have some fun with your ending. A reader may remember your sense of humor long after forgetting other details about you.

SUBJECT

Marni G, an obsessive reader of books, describes simpler days of childhood, when she had endless hours to read, read, read. Now, a hectic schedule permits only "small doses of my passion at a time."

GIFT

I hunger for an uncomplicated world where the Cat in the Hat is the ruler and Green Eggs and Ham the official meal.

SUBJECT

Debbie B's lifelong competition with her sister Michelle ended when Michelle left for college.

GIFT

. . . I stepped right into my sister's shoes (figuratively, not literally—because Michelle has a size five compared to my seven and a half). I think that my brain would become seriously warped if my feet were that squished.

2. End with an apt quotation, drawn either from the essay itself or from elsewhere.

SUBJECT

Craig S had to find safe shelter during a wilderness adventure.

GIFT

At that point I knew by instinct, "This is the place."

SUBJECT

Frank F had a part-time job in a hotel kitchen when a terrible fire broke out.

GIFT

To this day, whenever I smell food garbage, I hear the words, "Fire! Fire! Fire!" and the clang of fire bells.

3. Finish with a clear restatement of your essay's main point, using new words. Add a short tag line, perhaps.

SUBJECT

Carol B tells how she changed between ninth and eleventh grades.

GIFT

The main difference in me is that now I like myself. I could be friends with someone like me.

SUBJECT

Ian B learned about himself while reading Moss Hart's autobiography, *Act One.*

GIFT

There are no limits to the human spirit, no obstacles large enough to impede the attainment of a dream, provided that one's resolve and determination are equal to all the discouraging effects of failure. Further, there is no sin in initial failure. That's what I keep telling myself.

4. Bring the reader up to date or project him into the future.

SUBJECT

Sean N recalls his intellectual journey, trying to make sense of the theories of various philosophers.

GIFT

Almost every day I discover more about people. There is nothing, really nothing, more interesting. Fortunately, the world is crowded with them, and I've been given a lifetime to track them down. And if I ever get tired of it (I doubt that I will), I may just settle down on a little farm in some postcard-forsaken place and use the rest of my life just to think.

SUBJECT

Jonathan M hopes to become a well-known (and rich) artist.

GIFT

Someday, collectors and museums may want to hang my paintings on their walls. I am always hopeful. Nevertheless, I am playing the lottery this week. The jackpot is $20 million and the odds of winning are only one in three million. I hope the probability is more favorable in the art world.

Above all, avoid the summary ending. Trust your reader to remember the substance of your one- or two-page essay. To say everything again is not only pointless, it borders on being an insult to the reader's intelligence. Your essay isn't a textbook. A chapter review isn't necessary.

Some essays don't need an extended conclusion. When they're over, they're over. Even a short conclusion is better than none at all, however. At the end, readers should feel that they've arrived somewhere. In a sense, every well-planned essay prepares readers for arrival at a certain destination. The introduction tells readers approximately where they're going. En route, a series of ideas propels them toward the conclusion. At the end they're welcomed with a thoughtful gift. When they get to the last word, you don't want readers to say, "Oh, now I see what you've been driving at."

5 REWRITING AND EDITING

This could be the hardest part of writing an essay. You've invested a lot of yourself in the work by this time. You won't want to go back now and start changing things. Who can blame you? Try, however, to resist the impulse to rest. It's not time, yet.

Being tough on yourself is a courtesy to your readers.

Perhaps you're willing to alter a word here and there, check the spelling, relocate a comma or two, and repair a bit of broken-down grammar, but that's proofreading, not rewriting—and it's definitely not enough right now. Proofreading requires skill, but rewriting takes courage. It's painful work, for you may end up discarding large chunks of your essay and rewriting parts you've already rewritten. After you've struggled to get a paragraph just right, it's hard to give it up. Be brave. The next one you write may be even better.

Being tough on yourself is a courtesy to your readers. College admissions officials have plenty to do. You'll spare them extra work by doing all you can to make your writing clear. Readers crave clarity. They want to understand what you say. They won't do your thinking for you. Don't assume, "They'll know what I mean." Tell them *exactly* what you mean. By doing so, you'll improve not only the essay but also your chances of being accepted.

As you rewrite, deprive the readers of every possible chance to stretch, garble, or misconstrue your meaning. Here are some methods you might try:

> —Read your essay aloud. Your ear is a good instrument for detecting words that don't sound right.
> —Let someone read your essay aloud to you. Listen carefully, and watch his or her face for telltale signs of confusion or doubt.
> —Let your essay cool for a while—a few hours, a day or so. When you come back, try to read it with the eyes of a stranger.

The more rewriting you do, the better your essay is likely to be. On the other hand, you could write yourself right out of the essay. Too much painstaking revision may deprive the essay of its personality. The trick is to rewrite repeatedly but to make the words sound natural and spontaneous. Writers work a long time to perfect the technique.

Having Another Look

The root of revision is the word *vision,* that is, sight or perception. When revising, you *look again* to see whether you have said what you intended, and arranged your ideas in the best possible order. If you perceive a flaw or weakness, then revise—that is, *rewrite.* Read your essay ten, maybe twenty, times. During each reading, inspect it with a different set of lenses. Read it often for overall impression, but also to check it for each of these qualities:

—*Accuracy.* Have you answered the question on the application?

—*Purpose.* What do you want the reader to think of you after reading the essay? Have you portrayed yourself accurately? Does the essay sound like you?

—*Focus.* Have you limited the subject enough to cover it well in a fairly short essay?

—*Main idea.* What is the message you want to leave in the reader's mind?

—*Unity.* Do you stick to the point from beginning to end? Have you tied ideas together?

—*Organization.* Does your introduction draw readers into the essay? Can you explain the reason for the sequence of ideas in the body of your essay? What does your ending add to the essay?

—*Development.* What is the main point of each paragraph? What does each paragraph contribute to the whole? Have you said enough in each paragraph?

Finding Your "Voice"

In almost every essay that you're likely to write for a college, a natural, conversational style is appropriate. Since the essay should be personal, the language should sound like you—that is, like a thoughtful and well-spoken high school senior. When you use the pretentious language of a senator, the formal words of a legal document, or the slick style of, say, a TV commercial, you're going to sound like a senator, a lawyer, or a copywriter, not like an intelligent teenager applying to college.

So don't try to imitate anyone. Just let your genuine voice ring out. But don't confuse your "genuine voice" with everyday teen-talk or with an I.M. style of writing. It's not smart to cram your essay full of half-formed sentences, trendy usages, or pop phrases. Rather, consider the voice in your essay as the grammatically correct casual speech of someone who speaks well. As a rule, steer clear of writing anything that most students would feel uncomfortable saying aloud at a school board meeting or in a friendly conversation with a college interviewer.

> Don't imitate. Just let your genuine voice ring out.

Question: Can you find Becky's genuine voice in this passage?

> I desire so fervently to attend Amherst because I believe it is the only school that will enable me to explore my intellectual capabilities, heighten my perception of knowledge and gain a greater insight into myself and a greater understanding of others, in an atmosphere of united support for the individual.

No doubt, Becky wants Amherst, but she sounds more like a candidate for public office than a candidate for college. She conceals herself behind high-blown language that may sound important and profound but says very little—very little that's *clear*, at any rate. Contrast this with a passage from Lisa's essay about why she chose Wesleyan:

> During my visit in October, I had a good feeling about the academic life on the campus. It offers so much. I didn't want to go home and back to high school. Everyone I talked to in the dorm seemed happy about being in college there. If I am accepted, I'm sure that I will be bitten by the same bug of enthusiasm.

The voice you hear in Lisa's essay belongs to a genuine person. As she talks, you could be sitting next to her on the bus. Although informal, the writing is controlled.

You hear another kind of voice in this excerpt from the opening of Alec's essay for Columbia:

> You ask me to write an essay about myself. Eh? What can I say? Could Napoleon have written an essay about himself? Oh, what the hell, why not give it a crack, eh what?
>
> When I indulge in one of my favorite activities, thinking about myself, the word *unique* kicks around the old noggin. . . .

Alec sounds like a smart aleck. You'd never guess that he's a deep and discerning thinker. Later in the piece, however, he stops babbling and finds a more honest voice. Breezy it is, but no longer obnoxious:

> Enough about my intellectual musings (and what amusing musings they are). Another field of interest I cultivated in lieu of physical activity was acting. In the eight years that I have acted professionally, having appeared off Broadway and on a CBS movie of the week, I have basically developed into a character actor. However, I have been working on playing more natural parts lately, and even though I still play character parts, they have become less caricatured and more natural.
>
> Although I intend to pursue acting as a career, I don't intend to major in it. For two reasons: (1) I have other scholarly interests, and (2) I'm a klutz and could never wait on tables to support myself, so I hope to teach instead.

Here's another trick that could help you find your genuine voice: Write your essay in the third person, as though you were writing about someone else. Use *he* or *she* instead of *I*, *him*, *his*, *she* and *her* instead of the usual *me* and *my*. This technique often works because you'll tend to view yourself more objectively. Try to see if it works for you. Before submitting the essay, however, don't forget to change all the pronouns into first person.

To give your writing voice a final check, hand your essay to someone who doesn't know you. If a stranger can describe you accurately after reading your work, you can safely say that you've been faithful to yourself.

Editing for Clarity

You probably started editing your essay soon after composing the first few lines. That is, you changed and reworded sentences to make certain they said what you wanted them to say. As you continue, regard every word and phrase as a potential threat to the clarity of your writing. Ask yourself repeatedly: Is this the clearest word for me to use here? Are these words arranged in the clearest order?

Plain Words

To write clearly, use plain words. Never use a complex word because it sounds good or it makes you seem more mature. A college essay is not the place to show off your vocabulary. Use a so-called SAT word only when necessary—that is, when it's the only word that will add something to the essay's tone and meaning, which you'll lose by using a common word. Keep that thesaurus on the shelf unless you are stuck. An elegant word used merely to use an elegant word is bombastic . . . er . . . big sounding and unnatural.

> A college essay is not the place to show off your vocabulary.

Simple ideas dressed up in ornate words often obscure meaning. Worse, they make the writer sound phony, if not foolish. For example, you wouldn't say, "I'm going to my *domicile*" after a day at school, and you don't call your teachers *pedagogues*. Yet, this overblown sentence appeared on the draft of an essay for Northwestern: "My history pedagogue insisted that I labor in my domicile for two hours each night." How much clearer to have written, "My history teacher assigned two hours' homework every night."

Notice how clear these sentences sound when the inflated words are removed:

FANCY

The more I recalled her degradation of me, the more inexorable I became.

PLAIN

The more I thought of her insults, the more determined I grew.

FANCY

During that year, my proclivities toward blogging were instigated.

PLAIN

During that year, I became an avid blogger.

FANCY

I learned the importance of cordiality and cooperation in a competitive racing situation.

PLAIN

I learned that teamwork pays off in a race.

Please don't interpret this plea for plain words as an endorsement of everyday slang. If you need an expression like *pure dead brilliant, phat-phree,* and *KPC,* or a comic-book word like *gonna* and *gotta,* by all means use it. For heaven's sake, though, use such words sparingly and only to create an effect you can't do without. Don't highlight a word with "quotes" to signal that you know it's nonstandard. If, to make its point, your essay overdoses on slang, be sure to show your mastery of standard English by writing another part of your application in good, straightforward prose.

English is loaded with simple words that can express the most profound ideas. Descartes' famous observation, "I think, therefore, I am," reshaped forever the way we think about existence. Descartes could have used esoteric language to make his point, but the very simplicity of his words endows his statement with great power. Ernest Hemingway called a writer's greatest gift "a built-in, shock-proof crap detector." Hemingway's own detector worked well. He produced about the leanest, plainest writing in the English language—not that you should try to emulate Hemingway, although you could do worse, but an efficient crap detector will encourage you to choose words only because they say exactly what you mean.

Exact Words

It's often hard to break the habit of using vague, shadowy, and abstract words. If you want your ideas to sink into the minds of readers, however, give them exact, clear, and well-defined words and images. Almost always, exact words help you express exact thoughts. Since a tight, precise, hard-edged word has an unmistakable meaning, give the reader a *wooden bucket* instead of a *container,* a *blazing sunset* instead of a *beautiful evening, white-haired and stooped* instead of *old,* and a *Big Mac, large fries, and Coke* instead of *lunch.*

To write with exact words is to write with pictures, sounds, and actions that are as vivid in words as in reality. Exact words hit harder than hazy ones:

HAZY

Quite violently, I expressed my anger to the other team's player.

EXACT

I punched the Bruins' goalie in the nose and sent him sprawling.

HAZY

Skiing is a sport I enjoy, not only for the esthetics, but also for the art and skill involved.

EXACT

I like to ski, not just to see snow-decked pines and brilliant sky, but also to weave gracefully down steep slopes.

Of course, you need abstract words, too. Words such as *beauty, love, existence, nobility,* and *envy* stand for ideas that exist in the mind. The power to think in terms of *situations, concepts, feelings,* and *principles* is unique to humans. An essay full of vague, hard-to-define words and ideas, though, will leave your reader at sea about what you are trying to say. A student who writes about an "ugly" teacher, for example, sends a different image of an ugly person to each reader. If the teacher is *a ragged, slouching shrew,* the writer should say so. Or if the teacher's personality is ugly, the student should write *ill-tempered and aloof* or show the teacher shouting harsh threats at the hapless class.

Anticipate reactions to every word. Ask yourself, "Might readers understand this word in any other way than how I meant it?" If so, strike it out and find another.

Although exact words will always be clearer than abstract ones, a word or phrase with multiple meanings may often help to tighten your writing. Every time you mention *dinner,* for example, you need not list the menu. Be aware, though, that nobody will care to read an essay that forgot to come down to earth.

Clear Sentences

Short sentences are the clearest—sometimes. Use a short sentence to emphasize a point. Sometimes you may need long sentences to convey complex ideas, although a complex thought may just as easily be expressed in clear, short sentences. When trapped in a long, strung-out sentence, break it into a set of shorter sentences. Later, if necessary, you can put the pieces together again.

Now and then you may run into a long-winded sentence that suffers from paralysis. No matter how you tinker with it you can't make it move without damaging its meaning. Walk away from it and repair it later, or try a few manipulations. Here, to illustrate a stubborn case, is a rambling bit of prose that needs fixing:

> A sentence can be molded into almost any shape, beautiful or ugly.

> One of my biggest rewards has been membership in the Science Alliance, which was formed in my junior year, at which time the alliance members were informed by the chairman of the science department, Dr. Rich, that they could serve as mentors to fifth graders at the district's elementary schools to coach them through hands-on scientific experiments using advanced scientific methods and computer technology.

REMEDY

Break the long sentence into shorter ones.

RESULTS (Some Better Than Others)

One of my biggest rewards has been the Science Alliance. It was formed in my junior year. When the Science Alliance started, Dr. Rich, the chairman of the science department, informed students about a new program. The program made arrangements for members to team up with fifth graders at the district's elementary schools. We would coach the fifth graders on how to conduct hands-on scientific experiments. During these experiments the students would be taught to use advanced scientific methods and computer technology.

or

One of my biggest rewards has been the Science Alliance, formed in my junior year. The organization's purpose, according to Dr. Rich, the science department chairman, was to mentor fifth graders at the district's elementary schools. As a mentor for two years, I have coached boys and girls in the fifth grade on how to conduct hands-on scientific experiments using advanced scientific methods and computer technology.

Move words from predicate to subject.

The Science Alliance has been one of my biggest rewards . . .

The Science Alliance, formed in my junior year, has been one of my biggest rewards.

or

Combine ideas; turn less important ideas into phrases.

Formed in my junior year, the Science Alliance . . .

My most rewarding activity has been the Science Alliance.

Change nouns to adjectives.

Science Alliance work has rewarded me . . .

Change nouns to verbs.

Change verbs to nouns.

The formation of the Science Alliance . . .

Switch the focus.

The Science Alliance introduced me to the rewards of working with fifth graders in . . .

My school's science department chairman, Dr. Rich, introduced me to the most rewarding work, . . .

I got my start as a mentor in science after Dr. Rich formed the Science Alliance, . . .

Once you start such sentence manipulations, you'll begin to see endless possibilities. Sentences are much like clay. They're malleable and can be molded into almost any shape, beautiful or ugly. In the end, every sentence should stand in the form that expresses most clearly, accurately, and gracefully what you want to say.

Clear Meaning

In your writing, words must fit together like the pieces of a jigsaw puzzle. Sometimes a word looks as though it fits, but it doesn't. A misplaced word may produce a rather peculiar sentence. Take these, for example:

While running to English class, the bell rang.
Working full-time, the summer went by quickly.
When only eight years old, my father warned me about smoking.

These may not strike you as funny at first. Look again. Do you see that these sentences describe a weird world in which bells run to class, summers hold full-time jobs, and youthful fathers dispense advice?

The authors of these sentences have tried to join two pieces that don't fit. The grammar is flawless; the spelling and punctuation are perfect. Even the writers' intentions are clear. In each sentence, however, the parts are mismatched. After the comma in each, readers expect to find out who is running, who was working, and who is just eight years old. They don't. They're left dangling. (Hence, the name *dangling modifier* or *dangling participle* has been assigned to this type of sentence construction.)

To keep the reader from dangling, the writers might have said:

> While the boys were running to English class, the bell rang.
> Since Charlotte worked full-time, her summer sped by.
> When I was eight, my father warned me about smoking.

Relative pronouns (*who, whose, whom, that,* and *which*) may also lead to problems of clarity. Perhaps such words may not deserve a reputation as troublemakers, but like a black sheep in the family, they have it just the same. They've acquired their name—*relative* pronoun—from their intimate relationship with another word in the same sentence, called an *antecedent*.

A relative pronoun and an antecedent are related because one refers directly to the other. In this sentence,

> It's always my brother who is blamed for trouble in the neighborhood.

the relative pronoun "*who*" and the antecedent "*brother*" are right next to each other, about as close as kin can be. In this sentence,

> It's always my brother, now approaching his twentieth birthday, who is blamed for trouble in the neighborhood.

the phrase "*now approaching his twentieth birthday*" intrudes, thereby weakening the relationship, but the meaning is still clear.

You run into a particular problem with pronouns when you try to establish a tie between the pronoun *which,* for example, and a whole series of actions, feelings, or words, as in

> First we had lunch and then our guide told us the secret of the cave, which pleased me.

A reader might honestly wonder what was "pleasing." The cave's secret? The guide's spilling the beans? Lunch? That the secret was revealed after lunch? The pronoun *"which"* might refer to all or to only one of these possible antecedents. It's just not clear. To repair the sentence you might change it into something like this:

> I was pleased that the guide waited until after lunch to tell us the secret of the cave.

If another meaning was intended,

> I was pleased with the secret of the cave, which the guide told us after lunch.

Another sort of pronoun, namely the word *this,* creates similar problems of clarity. Any time you start a sentence with *this,* double-check it. Make sure it refers directly to what you want it to refer. This is advice you should not ignore!

Harmony

Writers, like dancers, strive for harmony in their art. Every hoofer, hip-hopper, belly dancer, and ballerina works hard to achieve grace and balance, and you can tell in an instant whether they've succeeded. So it is when you write an essay. All the parts must fit together. An awkward, incoherent essay—one in which the pieces seem unconnected—will leave your readers disappointed.

As you edit your application essay, therefore, read it over again and again—not until it drives you nuts, but almost. Check it meticulously to see if one idea leads naturally and easily to the next. Look for words and phrases that tie ideas together. (Turn to page 107 for some common examples of transitions.) In a harmonious essay, virtually every sentence bears some sort of reference to the sentence that came before. Such references might be obvious, as in "furthermore" or "for example." Connections are often more subtle than that, however, as in this pair of sentences:

> I have an idealized image in my mind of families that are close, loving, laughing, generous, and supportive.
> I wish that I could find *such qualities* in mine.

Notice that the italicized phrase in the second sentence refers directly to adjectives listed in the first.

Sometimes allusions to previous sentences are carried in the meaning rather than by a specific word or phrase:

> I had a hard time finding his house in the dark.
> I *picked out what I thought should be the address* and knocked at the front door.

In this example the italicized words establish a link to the idea stated in the first sentence. In the second sentence the speaker feels unsure of an address. You know the reason (because it's dark outside) only because you've read the first sentence.

Search your essay for transitions of all kinds. Whenever you discover three or more successive sentences without transitions, your readers may be stuck with a hard-to-read muddle. Before you do any heavy rewriting, though, try inserting appropriate transitional words, phrases, and sentences. Don't wedge one in where it doesn't belong, however. This could confuse your readers even more.

As you've probably realized, editing a piece of writing is a painstaking process. When you examine every word you write, it's easy to drown in a sea of minutiae. Therefore, it helps now and then to stop fussing over the details and to inspect your essay as a whole. Say aloud to yourself or to anyone within earshot, "The point of my essay is . . ." Complete the statement with one clear, straight-forward declarative sentence. If it takes more than a single statement, perhaps your essay isn't sufficiently focused. You may be trying to say more than you have space for.

> Now and then, stop fussing over details, and inspect your essay as a whole.

After you've declared your main point, try to say what each part adds to the whole. If any part doesn't contribute, cast it away. By attending to the contents of the whole essay, you are in a sense checking its coherence, determining whether all its parts work together.

An outline of your essay will help, too. Outlines needn't follow the formal pattern you may have learned in school, but the same principles apply. That is, all the minor pieces, when added together, should equal the whole. In the language of writers, every sentence in a paragraph supports the main idea of the paragraph, and every paragraph supports the main idea of the essay. You'll know that you have a well-structured, harmonious piece of writing when you can't reasonably remove a piece without causing damage to the whole.

Editing for Interest

Don't bore your readers. Admissions officials may ignore an occasional lapse in clarity and even overlook a flaw in grammar, but if your essay bores them, they could lose interest in both your essay and in you.

Like most applicants, you've probably led a fairly routine life. That's no reason, however, to write a routine essay. Fortunately, there are plenty of techniques for turning an ordinary piece of writing into a highly readable and stylish essay.

Down with Verbosity!

Never use two words when one will do. Readers want to be told quickly and directly what you have to say. Wordiness sucks the life out of your writing. Cut out needless words. Readers value economy.

(Stop! Go back to the previous paragraph. Do you see the unnecessary words? Did you notice that the next-to-last sentence reiterates the first? Yes, the statement contains only four words, but are those words necessary? Do they merely add weight—and no substance—to the paragraph?)

Your sentences, like muscles, should be firm and tight. Needless words are flabby. Trim the fat. Make your writing lean. As you edit, exercise your crossing-out muscles.

Brevity works best. Go through every sentence and cross out extra words. The sentence you just read contains nine words (forty-three letters). It could be trimmed still more. For example, "Cut extra words out of every sentence" (seven words, thirty-one letters). When the sentence was first written, it read, "The writer should work through all the sentences he writes by examining each one and crossing out all the extra words" (twenty-one words, ninety-seven letters)—three times longer than the trim, seven-word model, and many times duller. Yes, brevity works best.

In lean writing every word counts. One missing word distorts or changes the meaning. To trim your sentences, squeeze them through your fat detector:

1. Look for repetition. Then combine sentences.

FAT

In tenth grade I accepted a position at Wilkins' Fabrics. In this position I learned about fabrics and about how to handle customers. (23 words)

TRIMMED

In tenth grade I accepted a position at Wilkins' Fabrics, where I learned about fabrics and handling customers. (18)

RETRIMMED

Working at Wilkins' Fabrics since tenth grade, I have learned to handle both fabrics and customers. (16)

2. Look for telltale words like *which, who, that, thing,* and *all.* They may indicate the presence of fat.

FAT

Manicotti is a dish *that* I always enjoy eating. (9)

TRIMMED

I like manicotti any time. (5)

FAT

Jogging has been a wonderful activity, *which* has stimulated my body and freed my mind to think. (17)

TRIMMED

Jogging has been wonderful for stimulating my body and freeing my mind. (12)

FAT

The *thing* that made me angry was mosquitoes inside my shirt. (11)

TRIMMED

Mosquitoes inside my shirt angered me. (6)

3. Look for phrases that add words but little meaning.

FAT

At this point in time, I am not able to say. (11)

TRIMMED

I can't say now. (4)

FAT

The chef stayed home *as a result of* his not feeling well. (12)

TRIMMED

The chef stayed home because he felt sick. (8)

But here's a word of caution: While trimming words in yr SA, UR not alowd 2 txt.

A BAKER'S DOZEN SPECIALLY SELECTED FAT PHRASES—NO, MAKE THAT THIRTEEN SELECTED FAT PHRASES:

FAT	TRIMMED
what I mean is	I mean
after all is said and done	finally
for all intents and purposes	(omit)
in the final analysis	finally
few and far between	few
each and every one	each
this is a subject that	this subject
ten in number	ten
at the age of six years old	at age six
most unique	unique
true fact	fact

biography of his life	biography
in regard to, with regard to, in relation to, with reference to	about

Readers are too busy for sentences stuffed with fat phrases.

After your sentences are pared to the bone, look at what remains and get ready to cut some more. Although it hurts to take out what you worked hard to put in, the writing will be stronger, more readable, and noticeably more interesting.

Show, Don't Tell

The genius who invented "show and tell" realized that seeing a pet frog or a souvenir model of Grant's Tomb was far more interesting to an audience than just hearing about it. Since writers can't use hands, make faces, or dangle an object in front of readers, they must rely on words to do both the telling and the showing.

> Show more than you tell. Use words to make the reader see.

Show more than you tell. Use words to make the reader *see*. For example, don't leave the reader guessing about Laura's beautiful hair. *Show* how the breeze catches the edge of her silky, brown hair. Don't just tell about the garbage in the hall-way. *Show* the splintered glass lying in the oily water, the half-torn notebook, and the newspaper, yellowed with age. Don't just say you felt happy. *Show* yourself bounding down the steps four at a time, coat unzipped, shouting into the wind, "Hurray, I did it!"

TELL

After I won, I experienced a wonderful and unique feeling, which makes me want to win again.

SHOW

After I won, my sense of accomplishment grew with every handshake and pat on the back. My face ached from grinning so much. I knew that I'd be back next year to win again.

TELL

There is so much I have to do after school that I often don't even have time for homework.

SHOW

The busy part of my life starts at three o'clock: pick up Scott, my baby brother; piano lessons on Tuesdays at four; French Club; work on the newspaper; and tutor my neighbor in math. I don't have time for homework, not to mention working out.

When words show what you have in mind, the reader can see and feel and hear what you saw and felt and heard. It takes details—lots and lots of them—to make a sight or sound or smell as real for the reader as it is for you.

Of course, your essay would soon grow tedious—both to write and to read—if you showed every grain of sand on the beach. Be selective. Show readers the sights you want them to *see:* the gleaming sand and fragments of clam shells; to *hear:* the squawk of gulls and children's shouts; to *smell:* salt spray, seaweed, and suntan oil; to *feel:* stinging feet and sweaty, sun-baked backs; and to *taste:* gritty egg salad sandwiches and parched, salt-caked lips.

Although too much detail can be boring, too little is just as bad. A balance is best. No one can tell you exactly how to achieve that balance. You need time to get the feel of it. Like walking a tightrope, riding a bike, or doing a back flip, it becomes instinct after a while. The context, as well as your judgment of the reader's intelligence, will have to determine how detailed you need to be. To get the knack a little more quickly, study a written passage that you found interesting. Pick out both details and broad statements. Use the passage as a general model for your own writing, but give it your own stamp. After all, it's your voice the reader wants to hear.

Active Verbs

At some point you must have learned that a verb is a word that shows *action* or *state of being*. That's a fair description of a verb if you're learning grammar. To an essay writer, however, knowing that *action* verbs differ from *being* verbs is far more important. You need active verbs to stimulate interest. Since active verbs describe or show movement, they create life. They perform, stir up, get up, and move around. They excel over all other words in their power to pump vitality into your writing. They add energy and variety to sentences. As a bonus, active verbs often help you trim needless words from your writing.

Active verbs pump life into your writing.

In contrast, *being* verbs are stagnant. They don't do anything. Notice the lifelessness in all the most common forms of the verb *to be: is, are, was, were, am, has been, had been, will be.* When used in a sentence, each of these being verbs joins the subject to the predicate—and that's all. In fact, the verb *to be* acts much like an equals sign in an equation, as in "Four minus three is one" ($4 - 3 = 1$), "Harold is smart" (Harold = smart), or "That is some spicy meatball" (That = SSMB). Because equals signs (and being verbs) show no action, use active verbs whenever you can.

Being verbs are perfectly acceptable in speech and writing. In fact, it's hard to get along without them. Be stingy, however. If more than, say, one-fourth of your sentences use a form of *to be* as the main verb, perhaps you're relying too heavily on being verbs.

Substitute active verbs for being verbs by extracting them from other words in the same sentence. For instance:

BEING VERB

Linda was the winner of the raffle.

ACTIVE VERB

Linda won the raffle.

Here the verb "*won*" has been extracted from the noun "*winner.*" Active verbs may also be extracted from adjectives, as in:

BEING VERB

My summer at the New Jersey shore was enjoyable.

ACTIVE VERB

I enjoyed my summer at the New Jersey shore.

Sometimes it pays to substitute an altogether fresh verb.

I (relished, reveled in, delighted in) my summer at the New Jersey shore.

or

My summer at the New Jersey shore took my breath away.

BEING VERB

It is not easy for me to express my feelings.

ACTIVE VERB

I find it difficult to express my feelings.

BEING VERB

There was a distant wailing of an ambulance.

ACTIVE VERB

We heard the distant wailing of an ambulance.

Practice will help you purge being verbs from your sentences and add vitality to whatever you write.

The noun you employ as the subject of a sentence will often determine your chances of using a lively verb. Abstract nouns limit your opportunities. For example, you're almost compelled to use a form of *to be* in any sentence that begins with *"The reason,"* as in *"The reason I am applying to Colgate* is . . ." You have few verb choices, too, when the subject of the sentence is *thought, concept, idea, issue, way, cause,* or any other abstract noun.

On the other hand, nouns that stand for specific people, places, events, and objects take active verbs easily. When your sentence contains a subject that can do something—a person, for instance— you can choose from among thousands of active verbs. Anytime you replace a general or abstract noun with a solid, easy-to-define noun, you are likely to end up with a tight, energetic, and generally more interesting sentence:

ABSTRACT SUBJECT

The issue was settled by Mrs. Marino.

DEFINITE SUBJECT

Mrs. Marino settled the issue.

ABSTRACT SUBJECT

The cause of the strike was the workers' demand for higher wages.

DEFINITE SUBJECT

The workers struck for higher wages.

ABSTRACT SUBJECT

The way to Memorial Hospital is down this road.

DEFINITE SUBJECT

This road goes to Memorial Hospital.

Being verbs aren't alone in their dullness. They share that distinction with *have, come, go, make, move,* and *get.* These common verbs do little to enliven writing. Each has so many different uses that they creep into sentences virtually unnoticed. Use them freely in contexts where they fit, of course, but stay alert for more vivid and lively substitutes.

Active Sentences

Most events in life don't just occur by themselves. Somebody does something, somebody *acts.* Hamburgers don't just get eaten. People—Julie, Paul, and Mr. Dolan—eat them. Marriages don't just happen; men and women deliberately go out and marry each other. Touchdowns don't score, jails don't just fill up, graves aren't dug, cotton isn't picked, and herring do not simply get caught and stuffed into jars. People do all these things.

> To create interest, take advantage of your readers' natural curiosity about others.

The deeds that people do register quickly on a reader's mind. To create interest in your writing, therefore, take advantage of your reader's natural curiosity about others. Always write active sentences. Even those sentences in which no specific action occurs can be written in an "active," rather than a "passive," voice.

For example, consider who performed an action in this sentence:

> Six nights a week were spent in preparation for the concert by our class.

Clearly, the class acted. More precisely, it rehearsed for a concert, but the sentence keeps you waiting until the end to tell you who performed an action. Moreover, by placing "our class" at the end, the writer has been obliged to use the passive verb, *"were spent."* If you relocate "our class" to the beginning of the sentence, you suddenly activate the whole statement:

> Our class rehearsed six nights a week in preparation for the concert.

The change not only tightens and enlivens the sentence, it adds interest. You derive the same results any time you turn passive sentences into active ones:

PASSIVE

Every day, the newspaper was brought home by my father.

ACTIVE

My father brought home the newspaper every day.

PASSIVE

Rutgers was attended by my brother, my cousin, and three of my uncles.

ACTIVE

My brother, my cousin, and three uncles went to Rutgers.

Although active sentences are usually more natural, compact, and interesting, to avoid awkwardness you may occasionally need to use the passive voice when you are uncertain who performed an action, for instance, or when it isn't important to say:

PASSIVE

The blue curtain was raised at 8:30.

ACTIVE

At 8:30, a stagehand (or Mary Ann, a production assistant) raised the curtain.

In the passive sentence curtain time is the important fact. Who pulled the rope is immaterial.

Fresh Language and Surprises

Fresh language (1) stimulates the mind, (2) pleases the ear, and (3) surprises the emotions—all praiseworthy effects of a college essay. Dull writing, on the other hand, is predictable. That is, you can almost tell what word is likely to come next in a sentence. When readers know what to expect, they'll soon lose interest, both in the writing and its author. If you serve up verbal surprises, however, your readers will stick with you.

You don't need rare or unusual words to surprise your readers. A common word, deftly used, will do:

ORDINARY

I was ten before I saw my first pigeon.

SURPRISING

I was ten before I met my first pigeon.

Since people don't normally *meet* pigeons, the unexpected shift from *saw* to *met* creates a small surprise.

ORDINARY

The shark bit the swimmers.

SURPRISING

The shark dined on the swimmers.

Changing the verb *bit* to *dined* makes a common sentence uncommon, because the word *dined* suggests good manners and gentility, pleasures that few sharks enjoy.

Sounds can create surprises, too. Some words match the sounds they describe. The word *bombard,* for example, makes a heavy, explosive sound. *Yawn* has a wide-open sound that can be stretched out indefinitely. *Choke* sticks in your throat. *Murmuring streams* evokes the sound of—what else?

> When you surprise your readers, they'll stick with you.

A reader often derives unexpected pleasure from the repetition of sounds—either consonants or vowels—as in *"The dark, dank day smelled of death"* or *"The machine sucked up the sewage in the swamp."* You probably shouldn't repeat sounds too often because they may distract the reader from the meaning of your words, but an occasional treat for the ear builds interest in your writing.

Surprise with Comparisons

It isn't easy to find just the right word to express all you think, sense, and do. How, for instance, do you show the look a toll collector gave you, or how do you describe six-in-the-morning street sounds? What about the taste of sour milk, the smell of rotting garbage, the feel of clean sheets, a fear, a frustration?

> With comparisons you can express the inexpressible.

Writers often catch those elusive details and fleeting sensations by making comparisons. An original comparison will not only delight your reader but will provide you with words to express your most inexpressible ideas. In addition, comparisons are economical. They require fewer words than you might otherwise need to state an idea.

To describe old men in a nursing home, for instance, you could show their creased faces, the folds of papery skin at their throats, the pale, cracked lips, and the white stubble on their chins. If you don't need all those details in your essay, you could simply compare the men to slats on weathered wooden fences. Instantly your reader will get the picture. Yes, the rough gray texture of weather-beaten boards does suggest withered men lined up in a nursing home corridor, a likeness that probably hadn't occurred to the reader before.

Small children usually don't know enough words to express all they want to say. By nature, therefore, they make comparisons: "Daddy, when my foot goes to sleep, it feels like ginger ale." As people get older, they often lose the knack and have to relearn it. When you consciously seek comparisons, though, you'll find them sprouting everywhere—like weeds. Compare, for example, the taste of fruit punch to antifreeze, a sweet look to something you'd pour on waffles, a friend's voice to a chicken's cackle, the smell of a locker room to rotting hay.

Figures of speech, such as similes (Tom wrestles *like* a tiger) and metaphors (Tom *is* a tiger), are types of comparisons. They help the writer point out likenesses between something familiar (tiger) and something unfamiliar (Tom the wrestler). One side of the comparison must always be common and recognizable. Therefore, comparing the cry of the Arctic tern to the song of a tree toad won't help a reader familiar with neither water birds nor tree toads. Since most people know what a fiddle sounds like, a more revealing comparison would be: *The cry of the Arctic tern sounds like a fiddler tuning up.*

American English is littered with hundreds of metaphors and similes, once fresh and surprising, but now dried out and lifeless. Avoid these like the plague. *"Like the plague,"* in fact, is one you should avoid. Figures of speech like *"high as a kite"* and *"pale as a ghost"* have lost their zing. Don't resurrect them in your essay. Let them rest in the cliché graveyard.

At one time, every familiar combination of words, such as *"you've got to be kidding"* and *"I couldn't care less"* was new, witty, or poetic. Such expressions were so striking that people, thinking that they would seem up to date, witty, or poetic, used them over and over. Constant use dulled them and turned them into clichés. No reader will delight in a cliché. By definition, a cliché has lost its kick.

A TREASURY OF WORN-OUT PHRASES AND EXPRESSIONS TO BE AVOIDED

bummed out	would you believe?
how annoying is that?	go off the deep end
to touch base with	shag some rays
off the top of my head	for openers
try an idea on for size	flipped out
how does that grab you?	get off my back
the bottom line is . . .	off the wall
having said that . . .	no way, José
no brainer	many things on my plate
I'm getting psyched	It is what it is
I'm not a happy camper	I could care less
to think out of the box	

There are countless others to guard against. The number is *awesome*. They sneak into writing *when your back is turned,* when *your defenses are down,* and *when you least expect them.* Beware!

To avoid overused expressions, ask yourself whether you've ever heard or seen the phrase before. If you have, drop it, not *like a hot potato,* but just as quickly.

Sentence Variety

Monotony kills interest. A steady diet of mashed potatoes dulls the taste buds. A 200-mile stretch on a straight road takes the joy out of driving. Day after day of routine rots the brain. Listening too often to the same song destroys its charm. So it is with writing an essay. Repetition of the same sentence pattern makes readers wish they didn't have to read any further. Keep your readers awake, alert, and interested by serving up a variety of sentence patterns.

> Sentence variety keeps readers awake, alert, and interested.

Most English sentences begin with the subject, as in

> My sister got married last summer in a hot-air balloon 1,000 feet over Connecticut.

To avoid the monotony of many successive sentences in the same pattern, move the subject elsewhere and look for other ways to start a sentence:

> In a hot-air balloon 1,000 feet over Connecticut, my sister married her high school sweetheart, Jack.

After an initial prepositional phrase, the writer named the subject, "*my sister.*"

> Surprisingly, ten people witnessed the wedding—five in the same balloon basket, and five in another.

Obviously, the writer began this sentence with an adverb.

> When word got out about the wedding site, reporters hounded the couple for days.

After introducing this sentence with a dependent clause, the writer named the subject, "*reporters,*" and then added the rest of the sentence.

> Still, the ceremony itself was held without fanfare.

This writer snuck in the subject after an opening connective.

> To keep the wedding quiet, Jack and Annie kept the date to themselves until the night before the flight.

To compose the sentence, the writer began with a *verbal,* in this instance the infinitive form of the verb *keep.* Verbals look and feel like verbs, but aren't. At least they're not the verbs that groups of words need to qualify as complete sentences. Verbals come from verbs, though, which explains the resemblance.

> Drinking champagne, the guests flew for an hour before landing on a par-four fairway of a golf course.

Hoping to keep the reader's interest, this writer began the sentence with another kind of verbal—a participle. Very often the *i-n-g* ending indicates that you've used a participle.

> Thrilled by the adventure, the wedding party vowed to fly again on Jack and Annie's first anniversary.

Determined to begin a sentence with another kind of verbal, the writer chose a verb with an *ed* ending, which functions like an adjective.

Still another appealing variation is the sentence containing a paired construction. In such a sentence, you have two equal and matched ideas. Sometimes the ideas differ only by one or two words, as in: "*It wasn't that I was turning away from my family, it was my family that was turning away from me*" or "*While I put my heart into dancing, dancing worked its way into my heart.*" The strength of such sentences lies in the balance of parallel parts. Each part could stand alone, but together the idea has more muscle.

Once in a great while, you can create interest by reversing the usual order of words in a sentence. If used too often, the writing will sound stilted and unnatural, but look at the power you get out of a sentence that begins with an adjective that you want the reader to remember: "*Desperate I grew when the telegram hadn't arrived.*"

Likewise, an inverted statement—*"A math genius I am not"*—carries a lot more punch than *"I am not a math genius."* Use inverted sentences cautiously, though. In the wrong place they'll sound silly.

Lucky is the writer in search of variety, for English contains a huge selection of sentence types, many of which you probably learned about in school. Obviously, there are long and short sentences. At your fingertips you also have simple, compound, and complex sentences. You have declarative, interrogative, imperative, and exclamatory sentences. You can write sentences interrupted in midstream by a dash—although some people will tell you it's not quite proper. You can also use direct and indirect quotes, and once in a great while—to drive home a point—a single emphatic word. Perfect!

With so many choices, there's no excuse for writing humdrum sentences that march monotonously through your essay. Please your reader with combinations and variations. Don't mix up sentence types just to mix up sentence types, however. You may end up with a mess on your hands. Always be guided by what seems clearest and by what seems varied enough to hold your reader's interest.

A NOTE ON REPETITION

On occasion, skillful use of repetition enables you to stress an idea in an unusual way. At first glance, for example, this passage from Sally McC's essay appears repetitive:

> My grandmother raised me. She took pride in her five grandchildren. She introduced me to theater and ballet. She sat patiently through my piano and dance recitals. She sent me to sleep-away camp every summer. She did all a mother is expected to do except live long enough to see me apply to Smith, her alma mater.

Every sentence but the first starts with the same word. Yet, the paragraph isn't monotonous. What strikes you is not the similarity of the sentences, but the grandmother's devotion to child rearing. In this instance, Sally used repetition to her advantage.

Short and Long Sentences

Sentences come in all lengths, from one word to thousands. A long sentence demands greater effort from readers because, while stepping from one part of the sentence to the next, they must keep track of more words, modifiers, phrases (not to speak of parenthetical asides), and clauses without losing the writer's main thought, which may be buried amid any number of secondary, or less important, thoughts. Short sentences are easier to grasp. A brief sentence makes its point quickly and sometimes with considerable potency, as in this passage from Tracy P's essay about a trip to Florida:

> A balance of short and long sentences works best.

> For a day and a night the five of us—my parents, two sisters and I—sat upright in our van and drove and drove and drove. For thirty hours we shared our thoughts and dreams, counted McDonald's, told stories, ate granola bars, drank juice, dozed, played games on our iPhones, sat wordlessly, and finally, by the water in Daytona, we watched a brilliant crimson sun rise out of the Atlantic. But mostly, we argued.

The brief sentence at the end jolts the reader. Its bluntness, especially after a windy, forty-four-word sentence, produces a mild shock. Placing a tight, terse sentence next to a lengthy one creates a startling effect. The technique, however, works best when used only rarely. Overuse dilutes its impact.

Also, several short sentences in a row can be as tiresome as a string of long, complex sentences. A balance works best. If you have strung together four or five equally long (or short) sentences, separate (or combine) them. Here, to illustrate, is a drawn-out sentence in need of dismemberment:

> Because I was certain that it would be all right, without waiting for the approval of my mother, who was not yet home from the hospital after her operation for a back ailment that had been troubling her for years—in fact, ever since her automobile accident on the way to Chicago one Christmas, I decided during spring vacation to apply for a job as a counselor at a summer camp for children, six to fourteen years old, in Brookdale, a tiny village close to my uncle's farm in Wisconsin.

To lighten the load of an extended sentence like this, you could divide it, rearrange it, add verbs, drop an idea or two, change the emphasis, and cut words. You could employ some of the sentence-fixing tools described on pages 121 to 122. When you're done, the ideas, now clearer and more streamlined, might sound something like this:

> During spring vacation I applied for a counselor's job at a summer camp in the tiny village of Brookdale, Wisconsin. The camp, for six- to fourteen-year-olds, is near my uncle's farm. I was certain my mother wouldn't mind. So I didn't wait for her to return from the hospital, where she was recuperating from an operation for a back ailment.

Conversely, you achieve greater balance when you combine a string of several very short sentences. For instance:

> I live in two environments. I was born in Canada. I lived there for ten years. Then we moved to Boston. That was an important event. It was painful. The kids in Boston were cold and distant. All my friends were in Montreal.

Although the terse sentences may vaguely suggest the writer's despair, the writing style calls to mind a grade school primer. Greater fluidity and grace are expected from college applicants. The passage cries out for revision—perhaps something like this:

> I am from two environments, one Canadian and one American. I was born in Montreal, but moved to Boston at age ten. The move was painful. Cold and distant acquaintances surrounded me in Boston. Friends lived in Montreal.

Note that you frequently get a small bonus when you combine sentences: Your writing gets more active and less wordy—both worthy goals for a writer.

The Final Check

If you took the task of editing seriously, your essay should now be in very good shape, maybe in better shape than you are. Many writers, even the best, sometimes don't know whether their hard labor and sacrifice are worth it. They can't tell whether they've done a good job. Self-doubt is the writer's trademark, the price you pay for a clear, precise, interesting, and correct essay.

Although your essay may half-sicken you by now, stick with it just a little longer. It's probably better than you think. After all, you're not a professional writer so you shouldn't expect to write like one. High school quarterbacks don't play for the Dallas Cowboys, high school actors don't win Emmys, and high school writers—even the best of them—can't compete with the pros. Chances are you've written a decent essay that will stand up in any college admissions office. Your struggle to get the words right has probably paid off. You've revised and edited, re-revised and re-edited. Good! You added, cut, switched parts around. Very good! That shows you've been thinking. You logged plenty of computer time. You walked away, came back, tried again. Perhaps you wrote ten times as many words as you actually used.

Finally, you got the words the way you want them—the way they should be. You survived the ordeal, and the reader in the admissions office, who doesn't know you yet—but soon will—will be happy to make your acquaintance.

Before you send in the final version of your essay, check the whole thing one more time. Don't be satisfied until you can answer YES! to all the questions on this Editing Checklist:

	YES!	MOSTLY	HARDLY	NO
Does the essay *sound* like you?	❏	❏	❏	❏
Have you used *plain* words?	❏	❏	❏	❏
Have you used *exact* language?	❏	❏	❏	❏
Does your essay have *focus*?	❏	❏	❏	❏
Are all parts in *harmony*?	❏	❏	❏	❏
Is each sentence *accurately* worded?	❏	❏	❏	❏
Have you *trimmed* needless words?	❏	❏	❏	❏
Do you *show* more than *tell*?	❏	❏	❏	❏
Have you used *active verbs*?	❏	❏	❏	❏
Is your language *fresh*?	❏	❏	❏	❏
Do you include verbal *surprises*?	❏	❏	❏	❏
Are your sentences *varied*?	❏	❏	❏	❏
Is sentence length *balanced*?	❏	❏	❏	❏

6 PRESENTING YOUR ESSAY

Would you like to hear a sad but true story? It's about Scott, a high school senior, a good student—even a brilliant one—with a keen desire to go to Oberlin. Following the application instructions on the Oberlin website, he submitted the college's supplement to the Common Application weeks before he planned to complete the standard Common App. He wrote the essay for the supplement in less than an hour. He didn't give it a second reading, didn't proof it, didn't run the text through his computer's spell-checker. Frankly, he didn't even answer the question that was asked.

Oberlin's admission people concluded that Scott couldn't be serious about attending Oberlin if he submitted what they called a "third-rate" effort. In a word, they told him, "Forget it!" and advised him not to bother with the remainder of the application.

Obviously, there's a lesson in Scott's tale: Present your essay with pride, as close to perfect as you can make it.

Online and Paper Applications

Most colleges expect you to apply online. Some insist on it. (In 2013, when this book was published, plans were in the works to have all Common Applications submitted electronically.) To write your essay, use 12-point or 10-point type—nothing smaller. Also, use an ordinary font like Times or Garamond, similar to the print in this book. Avoid exotic fonts like Vivaldi and Pristina. They may look pretty but cannot be read easily. Double-spaced or 1.5-spaced text is preferable to single-space. You won't earn extra credit for fancy fonts or perfect calligraphy. University of Vermont's admission associate Susan Wertheimer urges students to prepare distraction-free essays. "Fancy graphics, tiny fonts to compress lots of text onto one page, or large fonts to use up space are often mere annoyances," she says. "You *do* want your essay to stand out but not for the wrong reasons."

> Most colleges prefer that your write your essay online.

If you use a paper application, either mailed to you from the college or one you've downloaded from the college's website as a PDF file, use high-quality white paper, 8½ by 11 inches. If the application leaves space for written responses, it is perfectly fine to print your words on a computer, then neatly trim the sheet and attach it to the application. But adhere to the instructions. Guidelines such as "Use only the space provided" should be taken seriously. So should word limits. Colleges mean business when they say, "Write between 250 and 500 words," or "No more than a paragraph consisting of less than 300 words," and so forth. Likewise, the Common App's 250–600 word range isn't just a suggestion. It's a command. (MIT says, "Yes, we'll count.") Some colleges may look the other way if you go over or under their word count by, say, ten percent. But be warned: Too many words (or too few) could count against you. If no limits or guidelines are given, consider the following: Admissions officials must read scores of essays every day. They don't have time to read lengthy, rambling essays. They want a quick take on who you are and what you value. Give it to them as succinctly as possible. An excellent rule of thumb is that two double-spaced pages is the absolute maximum. One and a half pages is even better.

> Don't write more than two double-spaced pages.

Also, number your pages, and if you write more than one essay, designate which is which by using the question number or by restating the topic from the application.

Proofreading

To proofread well, you need more than a computer's spell checker. You need fresh eyes. Your best proofreading method may be to let someone else do it. Print five copies of your essay, and have five reliable readers scour your piece for flaws in grammar, punctuation, and spelling.

If you're on your own, put your essay aside for a few days. Then read your essay slowly, once for the sense of it and once for mechanics. Read it a line at a time, keeping a hawklike watch on every letter, word, and mark of punctuation. You might even cut a narrow horizontal window out of a spare sheet of paper. Move the window over your essay a line at a time, concentrating

> Read your essay slowly, once for the sense of it and once for the mechanics.

on that line only. Search for missing words, extra words, and flawed grammar and punctuation.

By all means, use the grammar and spell checker on your computer, but remember that the computer won't detect misused words or words that sound alike but take different spellings: *there, their,* and *they're; its* and *it's; to, two,* and *too.* Also, such words as *principal* and *principle, stationary* and *stationery, whether* and *weather,* and dozens of others that trap unwary writers. Students using the Common Application face another potential pitfall, according to the director of admissions at Denison University, Perry Robinson: "They send the same essay to more than one college but forget to change the name of the college in their essays." Imagine the reaction of a reader in the Denison admissions office discovering that an applicant had "always wanted to go to Colgate."

Getting Help

Show drafts of your essays to people you trust—good friends, a parent, teacher, advisor, or college counselor. When you're facing a tough new assignment like writing a college essay, it's natural to seek a word of encouragement or help. Indeed, you're lucky to know people who can assist you. If you're willing to pay for help, go to the Internet. Dozens of sites offer editorial assistance for fees ranging from fifty to several hundred dollars, depending on the number and length of the essays and the type of service you ask for. Getting help from others, though, raises the impossible ethical question: When does your work cease to be yours and become theirs? There's a thin boundary between help and meddling. With luck, your well-meaning helpers won't overstep it.

> It's immoral and dangerous to submit an essay that cannot honestly be called yours.

If you've received suggestions for rewording a sentence or two, changing a few words, or clarifying an idea, you are probably still master of your own essay. If the help consisted of extensive rewriting, bloodying your paper with a river of red ink, and putting words in your mouth, you're about to submit an essay that cannot honestly be called yours. This is not only immoral, it's dangerous.

Books like this one feature essays that worked. Let them inspire you. Sample essays are often published by newspapers and magazines. By all means, read them, and let them trigger ideas for you to write about. Online Websites offer essays for sale or for the taking. With so many model essays at their fingertips, some students can't resist the temptation to lift all or part of an essay they didn't write, submit it, and hope for the best. Jonathan Reider, a veteran essay reader at Stanford, wrote, "You'd be surprised by how many copied essays we've seen. We once had two essays on dance that were clearly copied from the same source. To this day, we don't know what the source was, but we knew the essays were too similar to have been written by accident. We never would have noticed if we had received only one, but since we got two, both applicants were doomed."

People who read college essays for a living know the distinctive style of high school writing. Even the best of it differs from the writing of adults. Perhaps it's the rhythm, the use of a certain word, an unusual turn of phrase, the juxtaposition of ideas—each can tip off a reader that an adult has had a hand in the

> Get help, but not too much of it.

essay. There are certain usages that, although natural for an experienced adult writer, rarely find their way into a high school student's essay. (The sentence you just read contains just such an example. Notice that the subordinate clause, "although natural for an experienced adult writer," is embedded in the main clause. One in a thousand high school writers is likely to construct a sentence like that. It would be equally rare, too, for a high school student to say "usages . . . find their way." Teenagers usually don't express themselves that way.)

That's not to say that every ably written application essay will arouse suspicion in the admissions office. Many applicants write superior essays all by themselves. If a student with average English grades and unexceptional College Board scores submits a slick, highly sophisticated essay, however, a reader will notice. When admissions officers have reason to question the authorship of an essay, they'll scrutinize the applicant's school record and search through teachers' recommendations for mention of the student's writing ability. If they still have doubts, they may phone the high school for verification.

Getting substantial help with an essay may reduce your anxiety, but it also does you a disservice. You should make it into the college of your choice based on what you know, what you can do, and who you are. Misrepresenting yourself may get you in, but once on campus *you* will do the work, *you* will do the writing, *you* will sink or swim on your own. An essay that fools the admissions office will grant you a short-lived victory. In a few months, the real you will start bringing home real grades. Your application essay will be history, as will, perhaps, your career as a student at that college.

In Addition to Your Essay

Some colleges want more than an essay from you. They ask for paragraph-long responses to any number of questions—why you chose that particular college, which extracurricular activity you like the most, your favorite book, career plans, honors, and so on. Whatever your answers, write them with the same care as your essay. Start with drafts. Revise and edit. Use your most interesting writing style. Since space is often limited, get to the point promptly and express yourself concisely. Be attentive to the sound and style of your responses.

Some questions invite you to reply with a list of some kind—travels, prizes, alumni connections. If you can, respond with a thoughtful, well-developed paragraph. Not only will your answer be more interesting to read, you'll have the opportunity to emphasize the items that matter. Moreover, the reader will note that you took the trouble to write a coherent, lucid paragraph and that your writing repertoire contains more than just a college essay.

When an application asks, "Is there additional information we should know?" try to reply with an emphatic "Yes!" Since your essay won't have told them everything, grab this chance to explain more of yourself or to show your interests and accomplishments. Applicants frequently send their creative work—perhaps a short story, a collection of poetry, articles written for the school paper, slides of artwork, photographs—almost anything that fits into an envelope or small package. Don't overdo it, though. One carefully chosen term paper will suffice to reveal your love of history. One chapter of your novel is more than admissions people will have time to read, anyway. Submit only a small amount of material. When Tufts University invites applicants to prepare a YouTube-style video that says something about themselves, the time allowed is sixty seconds or less. As always, quality counts more than quantity.

Whatever you send, prepare it with the same high standards you used on your essay. Written material should be no less polished than your application essay; photographs and artwork should be attractively displayed and explained with captions. Before you send a CD of your music or a DVD of your gymnastic performance, make sure that it contains only what you want the college to see and hear. If you've ever posted photos of yourself on Facebook, written a blog about partying into the night or texting while driving, or engaged in any other activity that reflects poorly on your maturity and judgment, be sure to remove them. It doesn't happen often, but it's not unheard of for college admissions people to run across incriminating material about applicants online.

Don't feel obliged to create a piece of work just for your college application. Most people don't. It's not their style. Furthermore, most admissions officials realize that high school seniors have enough to do without the burden of an additional project. But if you have something on hand that reveals your uniqueness, by all means use it. For example, a girl interested in photography sent to Ohio Wesleyan a tasteful male pin-up calendar that she and a friend had marketed. A Tufts applicant sent copies of the school literary magazine she had edited. A young man who makes and sells intricate metal puzzles explained to the colleges why he sent one with each of his applications—"something to keep you entertained while reading essays." Two friends, both applying to Columbia, sent in a video they had made together. One aspiring architect submitted his blueprints for a geodesic-domed city with his MIT application. The Northwestern admissions office received a poem written on a jigsaw puzzle. To read the poem, the puzzle had to be assembled. It's not clear, however, whether it was ever completed.

> Don't go too far trying to be clever. Being yourself is your best bet.

Be creative, of course. Be serious if you're serious, witty if you're witty. Just don't go too far trying to be clever. Being yourself is your best bet.

When It's Done

What a glorious feeling it will be to click the "send" button on your computer or turn your application and essay over to the U.S. Postal Service. Then sit back and rejoice. Pat yourself on the back for a job well done. It's out of your hands, so relax and wait for the momentous day when the college sends you the good news by e-mail, or the UPS or FedEx driver delivers the *fat* envelope—the one containing information about housing, courses, freshman orientation, and, of course, the letter that begins, "It gives me great pleasure to tell you that you have been accepted in the class of . . ."

APPENDIX A.
ESSAYS IN PROGRESS

En route from first to final draft, essay writers often pause to survey the progress they've made. After writing each draft, they decide whether to continue as before, alter their course, or even start all over again. This appendix contains two sample essays somewhere on the journey to completion. Each draft is followed by notes on what the writer should do next. Notice that later drafts of each essay incorporate the suggestions for improvement. With more drafts, who knows—the writers may have produced essays to stir the blood of the most hard-hearted admissions dean.

Ellie E's First Draft

This essay responds to the "coming-of-age" question on the Common Application. Ellie wrote her first draft rather quickly—and it shows, as you will see:

> During an Outward Bound expedition in Minnesota I was put in several difficult situations. I never could have imagined them before. I was in front of a steep 80-degree incline and told to climb it to the top. My first reaction was, "There is no way I can do it." But I had no choice. I could not stay alone in the wilderness. My effort to climb the rock was the most ambitious I have ever done in my life. After two hours, I was up on the top.
>
> Even though I was there a short time, those two weeks were the most important of my life. My approach to life was different. In freshman and sophomore year I was put in many difficult academic situations. I was not making an effort. However, when I was in junior year, I made an effort. My motivation was greatly increased. Abilities I had never used before were now coming into use. My academic program was a challenge and I was meeting it gladly. With an open mind

and a willingness and a desire to try and learn, I enriched my knowledge and sharpened my skills.

I was in an honors English class with the name Modern European Literature. It was a large amount of work outside of class as well as in class discussion. The literature was difficult. I was taking the time and effort to read it until I fully understood it. In previous years, I would have dropped the class in which I was told I was going to learn about existentialism, a topic which I knew nothing about, and also write several analytical papers.

I was also challenged in math, which is one of my weaker areas. Math is not required for graduation, and I was against taking more than the least amount required to graduate. My strong dislike for the subject was keeping me from trying to learn it. But another part of me decided to meet the challenge. I didn't think it would be impossible if I made an effort. I soon found out that making the effort taught me the concepts, and logical thinking became easier for me.

Outward Bound also proved valuable in my employment. I was working as a waitress and a cashier. I had to interact with very demanding managers, co-workers, and customers. My patience was not unlimited. However, I could deal with the pressure and with others regardless of their personalities.

In the past year and a half I have shown that I can apply this new approach to my schoolwork and to everyday situations. Now I am ready to take on the responsibilities and challenges of college life and academics.

Notes to Ellie

—You have chosen a good topic, likely to impress a college, because it shows that you know what you are capable of once you put your mind to it.
—Maintain the premise of your piece, that is, how your experience in the Minnesota wilderness helped to transform you and change your attitude toward school and work. In fact, try to strengthen the cause/effect relationship.
—You attribute your sudden coming-of-age to a single climbing experience up a steep hill. That is not plausible. To change you so dramatically, there must have been more to the Outward Bound adventure. Try to give more details. What other things occurred during those two weeks to give you a new sense of yourself?

—Your essay has good unity. You never stray from your topic.

—A word about your writing style. Note that most of your sentences use "to-be" verbs. Enliven the writing with more active verbs, which will also tighten the prose and make it more interesting to read. Also, tie ideas together with transitional words. Finally, combine sentences. Too many simple sentences tend to give equal weight to every idea. Try to emphasize the ideas that matter most.

Ellie's Second Draft

I returned from an Outward Bound expedition in Minnesota shortly before I began my junior year. The return was difficult as I tried to apply my new confidence to my everyday life, including my education. In Minnesota I had been put into several difficult situations that I never could have imagined before. I found myself in front of a steep 80-degree incline and told to climb it to the top. My first reaction was, "There is no way I can do it," but I had no choice since I could not stay alone in the wilderness. My effort to climb the rock was the most ambitious I have ever done in my life. I struggled for two hours, sometimes almost giving up. I felt it might be better just to let myself roll down the hill and be done with it. I was encouraged by others and helped by the guide. I found the strength to go on. In the end, I stood on the top feeling like I had truly conquered the world.

Although I had been in Minnesota only a short time, those two weeks were the most important of my life. My motivation to succeed had greatly increased. Abilities I had never tested before were coming into use. My junior year in high school was a challenge and one that I gladly met. With my mind open, and a willingness and desire to learn, I enriched my knowledge and sharpened my skills.

I took an honors English class entitled Modern European Literature. It involved a large amount of work outside of class as well as in class discussion. Although the literature was often difficult, I took the time and effort to read it until I fully understood it. In previous years, I would have dropped any class in which I was told I was going to read long, hard books, learn about existentialism, a topic I knew nothing about, and also write several analytical papers.

I also challenged myself in one of my weaker areas, mathematics. Because math is not required for graduation, my strong dislike for the subject tempted me to avoid it. But another part of me decided to meet the challenge. I knew it would not be impossible if I tried. I soon found out that once I made the effort to learn the concepts, logical thinking became easier for me.

The Outward Bound experience also proved valuable in my employment. Working as a waitress and a cashier, I had to interact with very demanding managers, co-workers, and customers. My patience was not unlimited. However, I managed to deal with the pressure and work, regardless of the others' personalities.

I feel that in the past year and a half I have shown that I can apply this new self-confidence and motivation to my schoolwork and to everyday situations. Now I am ready to take on the responsibilities and challenges of college life and academics.

Notes to Ellie

—This is much better than the first draft. The connection between your climb up the steep hill and a more serious attitude in school is much clearer now. But it could be made even stronger and more convincing if you allude to the climb in your discussion of tough courses and work experiences.

—The paragraph on your work as a waitress and cashier is still pretty vague. Either develop that paragraph further with a brief anecdote about how you coped with pressure on the job, or drop it altogether.

—Keep trying to omit needless words (notice that you reiterate the fact that the reading in your lit course was difficult).

—Keep looking for ways to combine sentences and to provide transitions between ideas, especially in the first paragraph.

Ellie's Next Draft

For two weeks during the summer between 10th and 11th grade, I participated in an Outward Bound expedition in Minnesota. Out in the wilderness with a group of teenagers like myself, I found myself face-to-face with difficult, almost unimaginable situations. I never before thought of carrying a 60-pound pack for miles on a bumpy trail or paddling a canoe 18 miles in one day. These were huge challenges for me, because I am basically an non-athlete. Until then, most of the physical challenges in my life had been optional. If I thought that I couldn't run a mile in gym class, that was the end of it; I wouldn't even try. But in Minnesota I had no choice.

One day I stood at the bottom of a very high hill with an 80-degree incline and was told to climb to the top. My first reaction cannot be printed in a college application essay, but since I could not stay alone in the wilderness, I was obligated to try. My effort to climb the rock was the most ambitious I have ever made in my life. I struggled for two hours, falling many times, getting bruised, sometimes almost giving up. At times, I stopped and felt like it might be better just to let myself roll down the hill and get it over with. But I kept on maneuvering myself upward. Others encouraged me to keep going, and the guide gave me ideas about how to proceed up huge boulders and through narrow passageways between the rocks. Somehow, I found the strength to go on. In the end, I stood on the top feeling like I had truly conquered the world. My climb had been long and exhausting, but I had done it, and maybe for the first time in my life I realized that some things that at first may seem impossible can be achieved.

Although my adventure in Minnesota lasted only a short time, those two weeks were the most important of my life. I was in a coed group of nine people, some of whom I didn't exactly like. But I learned that everyone can get along if they have to and as long as they all try. Thinking about the experience, I probably couldn't have made that climb without their help, and they couldn't have made it to the top without mine.

When I entered my junior year, I found that my motivation to succeed was changed. What I learned in Minnesota I applied to similar circumstances at work and school. The Minnesota wilderness seemed to have changed my approach to life. During my freshman and sophomore years, I often faced difficult academic situations. And like the unrun mile, I barely made an effort. I had no idea what I was missing. When the going got too rough, my motto was to give up. I had neither the tolerance nor the patience to learn or to try new things.

In 11th grade, however, I took an honors English class entitled Modern European Literature, which involved a huge amount of work. Although the literature was often difficult, I made the effort to read it until I fully understood it. In previous years, I would have dropped any class in which I was told I was going to read long, hard books and write several analytical papers. I also challenged myself in math, one of my weaker areas. Because advanced math courses are not required for graduation, my strong dislike for the subject tempted me to avoid them. But the new me decided to meet the challenge. Remembering the steep Minnesota hill, I knew it would not be impossible if I tried, and so I did and soon found out that once I made the effort to learn the concepts, logical mathematical thinking became easier for me.

The Outward Bound experience also proved valuable in my employment. Working as a waitress and a cashier, I interact with very demanding managers, unpleasant co-workers, and impolite customers. My patience was not unlimited. Again, I think of my Outward Bound group and how we all learned to get along and help each other. That's how I manage to deal with the pressure of the work. Regardless of the others' personalities, I stuck with the job and saved a few thousand dollars to help pay my college expenses.

I feel that in the past year and a half I have shown that I can apply this new self-confidence and motivation to my schoolwork and to everyday situations. Now I am ready to take on the responsibilities and challenges of college life and academics. I thank Outward Bound for that.

Notes to Ellie

—Much improved.
—You have made a strong connection between your experience in Minnesota and your recent efforts in school. The contrast between you in 10th and 11th grade and you at the present time vividly shows what Outward Bound meant to you.
—The details of the climb have added life and color to the story.

—If you can do so very, very briefly, try to relate an anecdote about a problem with a customer, a co-worker, or with your boss on the job. If you add words, though, be sure to cut words elsewhere in your essay. At the moment, the essay borders on being too long.

—Some of the essay is still a bit awkward. Read your essay aloud and listen for odd-sounding words and expressions. For example, check the verb tenses in the next to last paragraph.

In this version, Ellie seems to have overcome most of the earlier weaknesses in her essay. Of the five comments in the latest note to Ellie, only two tell her what to do next. Evidently, Ellie has taken previous suggestions to heart, and her next draft is likely to be her last.

Chuck D's Early Draft

In this essay, Chuck tries to establish his identity as a fierce competitor, not only on a bicycle but in life. In fact, he compares riding a bike to living in a competitive world. The idea has merit, but in this early draft Chuck may have been carried away by the uniqueness of his metaphor. Without realizing it, he has presented himself as a rather unappealing and ruthless character. He needs to view his essay with a new set of eyes before going on to write the next draft:

> The large brown garage doors of a small split-level home slowly creak open. Out emerges a ten-speed bicycle accompanied by its rider. He turns and shuts the large doors. As he mounts his bicycle, a shaft of morning sun peeks over the treetops and glistens in his face. He squints and slowly glides out of his driveway. The race has begun.
>
> He moves slowly along the street where he lives. As he approaches his first hill, he casually shifts down to first gear. Slowly but steadily he ascends the hill. As the horizon breaks, he spies a small bicycle about forty yards away. Like a cat stalking his prey, he increases his speed, legs pumping like pistons. His prey is unaware of his approach. Suddenly, his prey glances back and sees him only a few feet away, but it's too late. Our predator swiftly passes his prey.
>
> Who is this killer on a bicycle? He is me. We are one and the same. Bicycling to school is more than just a means of

transportation. It is yet another test of ability. It is a need. It is a psychological contest. Who can get there faster?

Why is this so? I feel that we in the American middle class are brought up to be competitive. When I see another cyclist who I know is going to the same place I am, I feel that I must try to beat him. While I may accomplish nothing by others' standards, in my own mind I have overcome an obstacle. In my mind, to overcome an obstacle is an achievement. I also feel if one achieves the goals which he sets for himself, he will, in his own mind be successful. While beating another bicycle to school is a small achievement, it can give you the feeling, psychologically, of a big achievement, possibly helping to pave the way to bigger and better achievements.

What are the rules which we all must follow? What might happen if we break them? The rules are: Be cool. Never let someone know that you know you are going to pass. Surprise is important. If the person doing the passing were making a lot of noise about it, one of two things could happen: He could forewarn the other person and put him on guard, making it harder for him to pass, or he would cause the person being passed to feel resentful because the person doing the passing would be too showy. Always pass someone without their knowing it. If you are passed, try to regain your ground quickly. If you can't within a reasonable period of time, don't bother. If one did not follow these rules, it would most likely have an adverse effect. If you were to let someone know you know he is passing you, then he would only get that much more joy out of seeing you helpless, or at least unable to compete with him.

As you may or may not have realized, this essay is not about riding to school. This essay is about my love of competition. Bicycling is just an example that illustrates just how competitive our world is, or at least how competitive my world is. In high school it has been competitive, and I'm certain it will be the same in college, if not more.

Notes to Chuck

—Good, dramatic opening. If possible, build even more tension—the kind you might feel before an important bike race.

—The race itself doesn't really begin until the rider spies his competition. Yet, you say it starts when the rider hits the street. Which is more accurate?

—Several paragraphs start with questions. The pattern gets repetitious.

—The paragraph about rules is long, confusing, and repetitive. Do you need all those rules to make your point?

—You seem driven by a personal code of ruthlessness, creating the impression that you are selfish, suspicious and sneaky. Do you want a college to think that about you? Would you want to have a friend with those qualities?

—Don't explain the point of your essay, as you do in the last paragraph. Let the essay speak for itself. Make the point forcefully enough for the reader to get it without being told.

—The basic metaphor of life as a bike race is clear, but you haven't fully explained where else in life you have experienced such intense competition.

Chuck's Next Draft

The large brown garage door slowly creaks open. Out into the morning sunshine a rider on a ten-speed emerges. He checks his helmet and the leg of his trousers. All in place. He glides silently down the drive and onto the street, pedaling slowly.

At the first hill he casually shifts down, then slowly but steadily ascends the hill. As the horizon breaks, he spies another cyclist just swinging around the corner onto the boulevard. He increases speed, legs pumping like pistons.

The race is on. He's like a cat, stalking his prey. Slowly the gap between them narrows. His prey is unaware of his approach. Suddenly, his prey glances back and sees him. But it's too late. He's by in a flash, his vanquished victim left in the dust.

Who is this speedster? Who is this cheetah of the road, outracing everyone who crosses his path? It is me. I am the unconquerable one. It's in my blood to race, to overcome, to win, even when it's just the daily ride to school.

Bicycling to school is not just a means of transportation. It is a sport, a contest to see who is fastest. It's a symptom of growing up in the great middle class of America. We have been bred on competition. From Little League to class rank, from college boards to basketball, winning always counts as the only thing that matters. Who is fastest, smartest, tallest, quickest, most popular, strongest, best looking, sexiest, most likely to succeed? Win, win, win says the wind. So, whenever I see another cyclist, I feel that I must try to beat him. It may seem like I have accomplished nothing, but to me it is another achievement, another obstacle overcome in the race of life.

I feel that if you achieve the goals you set for yourself, even the smallest ones, you will be successful in your own mind. While beating another bicyclist to school may accomplish nothing, it satisfies my longing to excel, to feel psychologically that I am better, faster and more ready to face the world.

I don't feel this competitive urge when cycling with a friend. Friends are for getting to know, not for defeating in a race. In friendship there is trust. Neither you nor your friend should feel the other's need to compete. If they feel the need, then friendship terminates, falling as a victim of mutual distrust.

So, the rules of life are like the rules of the bicycle race. Never let someone know you are coming up behind him. A warning will put him on his guard and make the passing more difficult. If you are passed, try to regain ground quickly, but if you can't within a reasonable period, don't try unless you know you can do it. It's better not to let the other person see you in distress, for he'll only get more joy out of seeing you helpless, or at least unable to compete with him. Then he may toy with you, tease you by slowing down and zooming ahead when you think you will pass him.

Long ago, Charles Darwin called it survival of the fittest. That's the way it was and always will be as long as we live in a competitive society.

Notes to Chuck

—At the start, short sentences and phrases create tension. You've hooked your reader firmly. Good!

—You've made yourself much more likeable in this version of the essay.

—You show that your competitive urges come from society, not from some dark impulse deep inside you.

—The paragraph about friendship adds another dimension to your personality.

—In this draft, you make your point clearly—and without specifically telling the reader what it is. Well done!

—This essay is almost ready to send, but not quite. Read it over carefully for unneeded words and for repetitive phrases and ideas. For instance, in the second sentence, "out" and "emerges" are redundant. Using almost identical phrases, you mention twice (sixth and seventh paragraphs) that passing the other bicyclist seems to accomplish nothing, a disclosure that you should reconsider. After all, you don't want to give readers the impression that you have uncontrollable ambition or that you are hellbent to get your way regardless of the cost. Such traits will not be received well in college admissions offices.

After some minor editing Chuck's essay will be complete, and Chuck, being a hard-core competitor, will no doubt send it off confident that it will win him a place in the college of his choice.

APPENDIX B.
COMPLETED ESSAYS

When college admissions deans curl up to read a bunch of essays, they look for answers to two key questions about each applicant:

1. What does this essay tell us about the person who wrote it?
2. What does it tell us about how well this person can write?

The second question more or less answers itself when an essay presents a clear and accurate picture of the writer. You won't find many muddled *and* well-written self-portraits. Therefore, the impression you create rests largely on how vividly you are able to project yourself onto the page.

In this appendix you'll find three college essays. Each, for better or worse, reveals the writer's personality. Before you look at the brief analysis following each essay, decide for yourself whether the essay succeeds. Put yourself in the place of a college admissions officer. What does each essay tell you about its author?

Paul G

Paul, a high school senior, put on a pair of figure skates when he was eleven and has rarely taken them off since then. He is an ice dancer. He practices hours every day, enters (and sometimes wins) competitions, and dreams of skating in the Olympics. Ice dancing consumes a major portion of his time. To convince colleges that he is more than a one-dimensional person, however, he wrote an essay titled "Achieving a Balance."

> Achieving a balance on an almost paper-thin blade of steel can be a stressful experience. The first time I fell it hurt. I think of where I was then and where I am now and see my life in between as a balancing act, much like skating is, literally. The lesson I learned from falling that first time I remember: "If you stay balanced, you won't fall."

Over the next six years I learned how to stand; strong and confident. Now, spending hours a day training, I rarely, if ever, think about falling. In the beginning it was just another new sport. Now, ice dancing is a passion. However, sometimes a passion can become a misguided devotion to only one part of life. As competition and training became more difficult, keeping life in perspective grew more challenging. Increased skating demands forced me to get better organized. My mother and I spend hours driving to rinks, so I used that time to read a lot—from Cormac McCarthy to the newest Brian Jacques (a holdover from my childhood). Through it all I remained sane by staying in conventional school (competitors typically opt for tutoring or home schooling). I made time to spend with friends, continued to play tennis and baseball (despite some skating coaches' objections to playing other sports), and I rejected the notion that skaters had to live a life secluded in a rink.

My coach and friend Mikchail Zverev taught me what ice dancing really means: to skate with a partner as one and to feel each other's every move. I learned from him how to deal with inherently subjective judging by focusing on how well I skated, and then thinking about improving my skating even more. Mikchail's life in Russia had been harsh physically and politically. Because he had experienced what it was like to lose what you love, he grasped my need for staying centered—both on ice and in life. When the training got tough, he understood and helped me get through it.

There is a fullness in life that I have enjoyed because of my skating and what it has given me. But life is not all about oneself, and last year I was given a chance to start teaching a group of underprivileged girls through a program called Figure Skating in Harlem. The cold wind off the Hudson River could not diminish my enjoyment in giving back to skating. The smiles on the girls' faces, and on mine, when they achieved something new made me relish each Saturday.

Having the talent to skate has led to tough choices, but I think that trading skating for an easier, less stressful, life would have been copping out. I chose skating but rejected the baggage that too often came with it; a narrow view of life with too little exposure to the real world. The thin steel blade that had the potential to trip up my life instead led me to balance skating with learning, with other sports, with friends and family—all of which have enriched my life.

—*Paul G the person has considerable self-confidence and a sense of who he is . . . has a competitive streak in him . . . realizes the diversity that life has to offer . . . knows he has a special talent but has rejected the life of a celebrity . . . takes pride in helping others.*
—*Paul G the writer knows how to catch the reader with an appealing opening . . . has an original mind and the imagination of a poet . . . understands how to show his many-sided personality without writing a list . . . knows how to sustain a metaphor . . . realizes that an essay's conclusion should remind the reader of the introduction . . . shows facility in writing clear English.*

Peter S

At the start of his essay, Peter addresses the admissions committee directly. Writing the essay, he feels, is like fighting a battle with an unseen enemy.

It is hard for me to believe that the crucial time has arrived when I will leave the protective world of high school and enter another world as a major contestant and participant. Applying to college is my first step as a contestant in a unique kind of battle, one that is fought without blood—only sweat and tears. You, the admissions committee, become the judges. In your heads the decisive victories are won and lost. We, the winners and losers, battle one another only in words. Our minds and souls come to you in a record of scores, letters of recommendation, and, perhaps most of all, through this essay. Here you find out about the "me" not revealed in transcripts or through others' words. Each word I write represents another piece to the puzzle of my mind. How I sympathize with you, for some of the pieces may seem confusing or not even part of the puzzle.

Initially, I tried writing an essay that explained how I have been working to improve myself as a person. I grew frustrated with the difficulty of portraying the person I would like you to know, or finding an adequate way to show you my elation over the changes and growth I have experienced, especially since last summer. Now I can picture you sitting there thinking, "Well, here is another kid trying to get into our college by telling us how he has improved as a person." To tell you the truth, that picture makes me somewhat defensive. I know what this war is about: It's essay-eat-essay.

Do you remember when you feared that each word you put down would determine your future? If I had submitted my self-improvement essay, would you have been as deeply moved as I was? Would you have dropped your jaw and danced with excitement as I did when certain events happened to me? Let me try!

I have always wanted to be a more sociable person who, on meeting new people, did not retreat into a shell. Picture me *before:* One day I was stopped at a traffic light when another car pulled alongside. Inside were three of the most gorgeous examples of "pulchritude" I have ever seen. One girl about my age turned toward me. Horror! She was looking straight at me, checking *me* out just as I had done to her! I began to get nervous. Was there egg on my face? Was it April Fools'? Then the most embarrassing thing happened. She waved at me, and what's more amazing, even had the audacity to smile. My pulse went crazy. Was this really happening to me? WOW! I sure would like to meet her. But NO! I shriveled up in my seat. The light changed, and off we went into our own worlds, never to see each other again. So why didn't I wave back? Here was the opportunity I had been waiting for, and what happened? I blew it!

This experience turned out to be a valuable lesson. I began to think, "Is this the person I want to become?"

Many months passed as I sorted out many feelings about myself. During a family vacation in the White Mountains I began to realize that I had to change things that had been part of my personality for so long. I began to experiment with a "new me" during my hikes in the mountains. Each new person I met, I greeted with a hearty "Hello" and a bubbling smile. Not even totally exhausted hikers looked unfavorably at this cheerful, outgoing lad. Then it hit me! This lad was who I really wanted to be.

The new beginning: Back at the hotel I began to worry. I did not want to lose the person whom I wanted to become. I would have to work hard to assume his identity at all times. Trying out my new personality was not always successful, and sometimes the security of my old shell seemed very inviting. But then, *Success!*

I had always wanted a job in the dining room of this hotel. On the morning of our departure, I talked with the maitre d' about the mountains, about the hotel, about the dining room, about myself. No matter. Now, I knew what I was doing. I was communicating more easily, without my previous reserve. I was enjoying myself. More importantly, I *knew* there was no egg on my face! At the end of our conversation, I asked the maitre d' if he would give me a job, and you'd never guess what he said. He said, and I quote, "I would love to have someone with your personality working in my dining room!" Well, I hit the thirty-foot ceiling!

After reading this essay, did you? Probably not, for it was difficult to convey my feelings and my thinking. But I hit it. Even if my self-improvement essay did not captivate you, I know that I have, in fact, grown.

I cannot deny the past, nor do I want to. Now I feel ready to do battle. My ammunition will come from within, and any victories, as well as any losses, will be my own. I have waged a battle with myself, and I am winning. I am liking who I am. No matter what the outcome of this contest, I will keep on growing and evolving into the person I want to be. I want to hit those thirty-foot ceilings again and again!

—*Peter S the person seems a bit unsure of himself at the start . . . grows increasingly self-confident as the essay goes on, as well as in life . . . thinks that he's misunderstood—that people don't see the sensitive, complex person residing inside him . . . has a sense of humor . . . has the capacity to change . . . has the resolve to overcome personal hang-ups . . . wants to succeed . . . is sincere . . . has the courage to reveal his anxiety . . . is blessed with charm and a gentle disposition.*

—*Peter S the writer takes risks with words and ideas . . . knows how to project his personality onto the page . . . can use an appropriate story to make a point and develop an idea . . . focuses on an important personal issue . . . demonstrates overall writing competence . . . uses sentence variety and vivid images . . . gets bogged down in wordiness occasionally . . . knows how to write a strong and memorable conclusion.*

Betsy S

Betsy portrays herself with several brief glimpses into her memory. Although the images are separated by time and space, when taken as a whole, they become a finely crafted, unified self-portrait.

Certain experiences that I've had in my life have helped to shape me, along with all my schooling and all that I've learned from other people, into the person I am today. Some of them, although they may have occurred long ago, are still so vivid to me that I feel that I could shut my eyes and be there in those places again. . . .

I grasp the lifeline with my bronzed little ten-year-old hands and stretch my toes down to touch the cold Maine water. Today is beautiful, the water is calm and glistening. The boat leaves a trail of white bubbles behind it as it glides along. We were up at sunrise, Daddy and I were. At least we were up to meet the lobster boats as they went by and we got the first pick of the morning's catch. I had taken a before-breakfast swim and now my swimsuit hangs from the boom, drying in the wind. I turn my head back, lean under the jib, and wave to my dad who sits holding the tiller with his bare foot. My mother sits near him, reading a book, my sister is sunbathing, and my little brother is play-ing with the hermit crabs that we've adopted as pets. My father beckons me back to the cockpit and lets me take the tiller. I stand with my bronzed, proud little ten-year-old face gazing up, over the cabin, off at the horizon . . .

The tears flow down my face, faster still as I glance at my sister and brother, their faces tearstained too. It seems so ironic to me that, at eleven years old, I am standing in the most beautiful restaurant in New York, in the most elegant dress I've ever owned, and I am experiencing the most pain I've ever felt. My father glances over his shoulder at us, even as the ceremony is taking place, and I see the pain in his eyes too. I think of my mother, alone at home, in the huge, new house that he just bought for us. What will she have done when he drops us off tonight? Last weekend she tore up their wedding picture. She's broken some dishes and called him every rotten name right in front of me. Inside I've called him them too. I'm only eleven years old and I'm so confused. I love my parents both so much and I'm not ready to have these feelings. I hardly even know this woman he's marrying . . .

I wake up, having slept for the shortest four hours of my life and I force my eyes open and I crawl to the shower as I shampoo my hair. My brain begins to function again and I think to myself, "Any sane person is going to the beach today, sleeping until noon, and wouldn't think of touching a schoolbook." After my shower, I go back to my room and Lindsey, my roommate from Toronto, and I get dressed in a hurry. Grabbing our books we run down the stairs and out the door of our dorm to walk to breakfast. On the way to the Commons, we begin to meet all our friends. It has become a daily ritual, these past weeks at Andover. First we see the kids from Stevens East and Taylor Hall hiking up the hill. Soon we see Jennifer and Dana coming across the quad from Day Hall. We walk into the Commons, grab some Cap'n Crunch and a glass of O.J. and walk over to join the others at a table. I sit back and listen to everyone. They're complaining about their homework, the lack of sleep, the food, the strict curfews, and chattering about our next trip to Boston, letters from home, the newest couple, and I smile at Lindsey and our looks say to each other, "When have we ever been this happy before?" . . .

I stand at the top and lift my face up toward the sun. I take off my sunglasses and lean forward onto my poles. I feel every muscle in my body, every muscle in my legs, my shoulders, my arms . . . A pacific, white sea lies in front of me. There's not another person around me. I'm skiing better than I ever have before. I'm concentrating on every move as if in slow motion. I feel so close to Heaven and so down to Earth. I feel a remarkable energy, maybe from the sun, maybe from the center of the Earth, flowing through me, making me glow. Everything inside me, in my head, seems to come together and I am whole. I lift my face toward the sun and I can't help but smile as I think to myself, "This is me. This is what I am."

There are so many other examples that I could choose to show who I am, many of them are not vivid images of memorable moments, but everyday parts of my life. I love to walk down the hall at school, talking and joking with almost everyone I pass, teachers and students alike. I love the feeling I get when I tutor someone and I help them to understand a concept that they couldn't quite get on their own. Most of all, I love to sit at the kitchen table and talk with my mother and her fiancé, or to go out with my close friends and laugh and hug and know that we can always lean on each other. I work hard and I play hard. I spend a great deal of time studying my books, but also a lot of time forming relationships with other people. I want all the beauty that life can give . . . all the knowledge, all the love. So I fill up my cup and I drink it in.

—*Betsy S the person loves life and appreciates its possibilities . . . feels and thinks deeply . . . searches below the surface for the essential meaning of everyday occurrences.*
—*Betsy S the writer has a rare gift for saying what she thinks and feels . . . has composed an essay that deserves to be read again and again.*

APPENDIX C.
STUDENT CONTRIBUTORS*

The dozens of students who consented to have some or all of their application essays reprinted throughout this book attended the following New York State high schools:

Horace Greeley (Chappaqua), John Jay (Cross River), Mahopac, Mamaroneck, Scarsdale, and White Plains.

Also, the Berkshire School in Sheffield, Massachusetts, and San Lorenzo (California) High School.

Elissa Greenberg Adair, Princeton

Chandra Bendix, MIT

Cheryl Berganos, Cal State (East Bay)

Joel Berkowitz, University of Pennsylvania

Ian Biederman, Northwestern

Deborah Brause, Tufts

Courtney Chang, University of California, Davis

Brian Cunnie, University of Pennsylvania

Peter Davis, Johns Hopkins

Roger Denny, Columbia

Teresa DiMagno, SUNY Binghamton

Charles DiMicco, SUNY Albany

Sabrina Eaton, University of Pennsylvania

Ellie Ehrenhaft, Ithaca

Susan Epstein, Yale

Lisa Estreich, Harvard

Susan Faulkner, Brown

Ellen Gamerman, Swarthmore

Paul Goldner, Harvard

Janelle Gonzalez, University of California, Santa Cruz

Alicia Grant, SUNY Binghamton

Maria Guarino, Fordham

Alexander Harrington, Columbia

Lawrence Harris, Franklin and Marshall

Eric Hecker, University of Pennsylvania

Elizabeth Humphrey, Fordham

Alison Lipow, University of North Carolina

Thomas Mackenzie, University of Colorado

Steven Maddox, Harvard

Jon Martin, Cornell

Sally McCauley, Smith

Pamela Meadow, University of Pennsylvania

Janine Clare Mendiomo, Chabot Community College

David Miles, University of California, Berkeley

Michael Miller, New York University

Tracy Parker, Carleton

James Reilly, Duke

Annette Rogers, Boston University

Elizabeth Schmidt, University of Michigan

Peter Scotch, Connecticut College

Andrew Smith, Washington University

Gina Smith, Syracuse

Linda Wiereck, Oberlin

*Several contributors chose to withhold their names
or to be listed under a pseudonym.

NOTES

NOTES

NOTES

BARRON'S COLLEGE GUIDES
AMERICA'S #1 RESOURCE FOR EDUCATION PLANNING

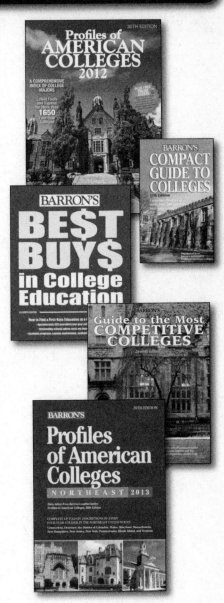

PROFILES OF AMERICAN COLLEGES, 30th Edition

Includes FREE ACCESS to Barron's web-based college search engine

Every accredited four-year college in the United States is profiled, and readers are directed to a Barron's Web site featuring a college search engine that presents exclusive online information to help students match their academic plans and aptitudes with the admission requirements and academic programs of each school. The book presents profiles of more than 1,650 colleges.
ISBN: 978-0-7641-4784-5, $28.99, *Can$32.99*

COMPACT GUIDE TO COLLEGES, 17th Edition

A concise, fact-filled volume that presents all the essential facts about 400 of America's best-known, most popular schools. Admissions requirements, student body, faculty, campus environment, academic programs, and so much more are highlighted.
ISBN: 978-0-7641-4487-5, $10.99, *Can$12.99*

BEST BUYS IN COLLEGE EDUCATION, 11th Edition

Lucia Solorzano
Here are detailed descriptions—with tuitions and fees listed—of 300 of the finest colleges and universities in America judged on a value-for-your-dollar basis.
ISBN: 978-0-7641-4521-6, $21.99, *Can$26.50*

GUIDE TO THE MOST COMPETITIVE COLLEGES, 7th Edition

Barron's latest and most innovative college guide describes and examines more than 80 of America's top schools. What makes this guide unique is its special "insider" information about each school including commentaries on faculty, and more.
ISBN: 978-0-7641-4599-5, $23.99, *Can$28.99*

PROFILES OF AMERICAN COLLEGES: THE NORTHEAST, 20th Edition

Comprehensive data specifically for students interested in schools in Connecticut, Delaware, D.C., Maine, Maryland, Massachusetts, New Hampshire, New Jersey, New York, Pennsylvania, Rhode Island, or Vermont.
ISBN: 978-0-7641-4749-4, $16.99, *Can$19.50*

Prices subject to change without notice.

BARRON'S EDUCATIONAL SERIES, INC.
250 Wireless Blvd., Hauppauge, N.Y. 11788
Call toll-free: 1-800-645-3476

In Canada:
Georgetown Book Warehouse
34 Armstrong Ave., Georgetown, Ontario L7G 4R9
Call toll-free: 1-800-247-7160

(#8) R 5/12

——————— To order ———————
Available at your local book store
or visit **www.barronseduc.com**